Kindness

Child Author Project

Kindness

A Project by Jessica Prime
Illustrations by Kate Worrall

ISBN 978-1-9160686-2-9

Format and typeset by Jen Parker at Fuzzy Flamingo
www.fuzzyflamingo.co.uk

Illustrations and artwork by Kate Worrall
www.kateprime.co.uk

www.childauthorproject.com

I dedicate this book to anyone in the world who needs a bit of kindness. Kindness makes the world a better place, but sometimes, it can be hard to come by. I hope that this book can be a ray of sunshine on a cloudy day. And, I dedicate this book to those of you who share kindness with others; you are my favourite kind of people!

Thank you to all the children who have taken part in this book project, you are all an inspiration and should be mighty proud of yourselves! Thank you for taking part, for sharing your thoughts, and for inspiring me with your imaginations.
You are all incredible!

Welcome

Child Author Project was set up to encourage the creativity, passion and imagination in children. As a child, I dreamt of the day that I would become an author; I dreamt that someday people would read my words and feel inspired.

In 2018, I became a #1 best-selling author, and I realised that I wanted to share the opportunity of being an author with young people.

With a passion for mental health and a dream to inspire and motivate children, Child Author Project was born.

Each project aims to open the door for conversations about mental health and emotion. The first project focused on 'Happiness', followed by this 'Kindness' project. These topics mean something different to everyone, and I believe we can learn a lot from what children have to say about these topics.

I wanted this project to encourage families to be open about mental health, and to show children that they really can achieve amazing things by being creative, passionate and by working hard.

In Support

Child Author Project is passionate about giving back to the community. The 'Kindness' book project is a proud sponsor of 'My Mental Health Rocks' campaign, a project that aims to promote well-being and resilience in children, whilst raising awareness of children's mental health.

My Mental Health Rocks facilitate workshops and provide resources to schools and communities across the UK and are growing worldwide.

Contact My Mental Health Rocks:
www.mymentalhealthrocks.com

With Thanks

Child Author Project would like to say a massive thank you to our corporate sponsors.

Ben Calder at Centre for Integral Health
www.bencalder.co.uk

Jo Howarth at The Happiness Club
www.thehappinessclub.co.uk

Esther O'Brien at Esther The Investor
www.esthertheinvestor.co.uk

Adele Potts at Phantastic Oils
www.facebook.com/phantasticoils

Alex Preston at The Bottle Top Notts
www.thebottletopnotts.co.uk

Laura Goodsell at Anchor Online Designs
www.anchoronline.co.uk

Annette Chester at Wholehearted Parenting
www.facebook.com/
WholeheartedParentingWithDrAnnette

Tina Stepney at Crafty Blues
www.craftyblues.co.uk

Louise McEwan at Mum & Son Adventures
www.mumandsonadventures.com

Nicola Reynolds at Hubbaty and Pixie Box
www.hubatty.com
www.pixie-box.co.uk

Joelle Byrne
www.joellebyrne.com

Contents

Child Author Project is proud to introduce:

Kindness

1. Seren

Kindness is yellow.

Kindness is a colour.

Kindness is the best!

***

Seren Mai Rees
Age 3
Carmarthenshire, UK

2. Skye

How to be Kind

When people are feeling down, you should help them because that's kind. When someone is feeling angry, you should help them become calm and happy because it's kind. When someone is feeling sad, you should say you can join in with our game because it's kind. When Lotte is feeling lonely, you should say, "It's alright, Lotte", and ask if she wants a hug because it's kind. When your cat is scared of something, you should stroke it to help it feel better because it's kind.

I love being kind. It makes me feel happy and helpful. Yay!

***

Skye Forshaw
Age 6
Merseyside, UK

3. Lotte

My Mummy and Daddy are kind because they always make me laugh all the time and give us big hugs and give me peanut butter!

Skye is kind, she shares her toys and she hugs me when I hurt myself.

I am kind because I love jumping in muddy puddles and I stroke my cats gently.

My cats are kind because they love me and meow at me every day!

***

Lotte Forshaw
Age 3
Merseyside, UK

4. Oliver

The Big Woods

There once were two boys called Jony Wollerway and Ron Henry, who were the same age as you are now.

They went to the big woods because they wanted to explore the nature, but Ron ran away; he tripped over and he got stuck in a fallen root in the ground, he fell over and landed in the mud. He was very sad because his leg hurt, but a nice stranger who was walking his dog helped him up and asked if he was OK, the man knew Ron's dad and phoned him for help.

Then Ron's parents came and put him in their car, they took him to the hospital because he had broken his leg.

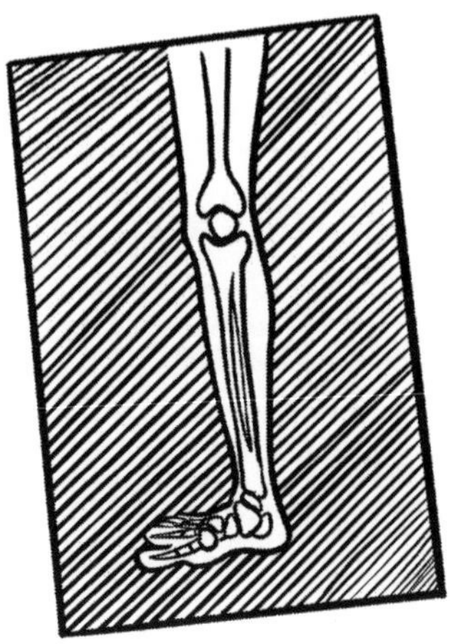

At the hospital the doctors x-rayed Ron's leg, they gave him some pain medicine and put his leg in a cast; they were very nice, friendly people.

All of these people helped Ron in the way they could, and they did it because they have kind hearts and care about people.

Ron was really happy that all these people cared about him and he felt loved, he understood that it is good to be kind to others and makes you feel all warm and happy inside.

***

Oliver Carter
Age 8
Leicestershire, UK

5. Alfie

Be Kind

I am kind to my friends, they are kind to me, we play together and share our toys.

My school tells me about kindness, it's part of our CARE code:

Cooperation
Awareness
Respect
Enjoyment.

I love my family and share my toys with my brother, I also like drawing him nice pictures.

It is nice to be kind to people by:

- Making friends
- Saying kind words
- Playing with them
- Hugging a sad friend
- Sharing is kind
- Saying please and thank you is nice
- Smiling when someone is sad

Kind
In
Nice
Dreaming
Nature
Enjoy
Sharing
Smiling

***

Alfie Carter
Age 5
Leicestershire, UK

6. James

"Warm and Fuzzy"

In his eyes I saw he was helpless. I felt sad for the man who was hungry and homeless.

I wanted to give him a home, food and water. I chose a sandwich for him and this made me feel warm and fuzzy, happy and good.

I gave him the sandwich. He was smiling and said, "Thank you, young man".

I felt amazing and liked him a lot.

***

James Gabriel Welch
Age 9
Nottinghamshire, UK

7. Sonny

Kindness

It's important to be kind to people, and then they are kind back, and that makes the world go round.

It's important to be kind to unkind people because they need it the most.

Some examples of kindness are;

- Getting someone a cup of tea
- Sharing your toys
- Saying "Are you OK?" when someone falls over
- Doing things for other people
- Cleaning your parent's car
- Being friendly

***

Sonny Collins
Age 8
Devon, UK

8. Olivia

What 'Kindness' means to me

It means showing respect for others.
It means love, friendship and caring.

Here are some ideas of how I think you can show kindness;

- Help people in need.
- Say sorry if you do something wrong.
- Send food to charities so nobody goes hungry.
- Share an answer or help if someone is stuck.
- Help someone up if they fall over.
- If I saw someone who was homeless, I would ask Mummy for some money so they could buy something they need.
- If someone lost a pet, I would help them search and we'd hopefully find it.
- If something sad had happened to someone, I would try to cheer them up and not remind them of their sadness.
- Say nice words.
- Remind people of the nice things about themselves.

I like to show Mummy and Daddy kindness by giving them huggles and kisses. When I'm sad, some grown-ups show me kindness; They help me if I fall over, to solve problems, to feel happier and by teaching me new things.

In October, we wore yellow to school to support mental health. I took £2 in; Mummy gave me £1 but I added £1 of my own money too. Everybody has mental health, but some suffer with it much worse than others. I have; sometimes I've been so upset that I get pains in my tummy. I want to show kindness to others who might feel like I have and help them to feel better and happier.

***

Olivia Preston
Age 8
Shropshire, UK

9. Phoebe

What 'Kindness' means to me;

If someone is sad, I'll go help them and cheer them up by being friends with them and being kind with them, not cross.

If someone fell over, I would help them up.

I like it when people say nice words and are sweet to me, so I will be the same with others.

At home, I like to be kind to Mum, Dad, Olivia (my sister) and my dogs. I like to be silly and do funny faces to make them all laugh. It's kind to show everyone I love them and give them lots of hugs.

It's kind to read stories to everyone and to write them nice notes and letters.

It's kind to share toys and play with people all together, it's kind to be helpful.

My teachers, dinner ladies and my friends are kind to me.

My mummy and daddy are kind.

Doctors and the police are always kind.

My bunny teddy is kind because she never wakes me up at night-time and if I'm sad she makes me smile.

My friend helped make me make a bird's nest at school – she was kind.

We should all be kind to nature because it is interesting, and we don't want to wreck it.

I am kind to animals, and people and if someone is kind to me, I feel excited.

Friends and family should be kind to each other.

Being kind makes people happy, we should all be kind.

***

Phoebe Preston
Age 5
Shropshire, UK

10. Katie

Kindness is everything, if you are kind to someone it will make their day and they will be kind to someone else and that kindness passes on and on. Kindness is contagious.

People don't understand how much of an impact kindness has on people if they are really upset or maybe angry. For example, if nobody let them sit next to them in lunch and nobody wanted to play with them and then someone let them sit next to them and play with them, that would be an act of kindness. Kindness impacts people in an absolutely amazing way.

If you are mean to someone it is also contagious, but in a very bad way. If you are mean to someone, they will pass on the meanness and it will result in them having a bad day, so make sure you are kind to people and treat others the way you want to be treated.

***

Katie Nicola Brown
Age 10
Northumberland, UK

11. Amber

The Kindness Cake Recipe

INGREDIENTS:
200g of smiles
200g of sweetness
200g of compassion
2 hugs
A dash of consideration

METHOD: Mix all the ingredients well and bake with warmth until ready. Ice the top with selflessness and sprinkle with friendliness. Then serve with a side of love.

***

Amber Alice Fowlie
Age 10
Aberdeenshire, UK

12. Millie-Rose

Kindness starts with me and then you.

It's cool to be kind, so never be mean. If you can't be nice maybe just don't be mean.

Be happy and friendly as it makes people smile. Do kind things for people, think of others for a while.

I really love our planet, so please be kind to it. Don't throw rubbish on the ground or in the sea because it will destroy it.

The people and the animals mean a lot to us. Walk where you can instead of a car, train or bus.

Recycle where you can and think about the things you buy. Get stuff without plastic, I think we should all try.

If we all worked hard together and made unkindness zero. We could save the planet; we could be the world's hero.

Sprinkle kindness around and bring happiness to the world.

***

Millie-Rose Hyder-Shepherd
Age 6
Kent, UK

13. Dylan

Once upon a time, there were a group of snow leopard friends out playing, one called Suma, one called Will and one called Indie. They were playing the game Hide & Seek.

Suma and Indie were hiding, and Will was counting. He counted to ten and then went to search for them.

Behind a rock, Will found Indie hiding quite quickly but he couldn't find Suma.

So, they both were trying to find their friend for ages!

Eventually they found him crying behind a really big tree. Suma had injured himself and hurt his tail.

Will and Indie pulled Suma to his feet and helped him walk home.

When they went back to Suma's house later to check how he was, they had taken him a cake that they baked together putting his favourite chocolate treat on top!

Suma's mum came into the lounge and she was amazed by the cake. She said, "Have you had a nice time with your friends Suma despite injuring yourself?" and he replied,

"Yes, it was lots of fun, but I prefer the cake!" He added, "I am glad my tail is all better now."

Everyone smiled and Suma said, "Thanks so much for being so kind to me Will and Indie."

Will and Indie replied, "You're very welcome!"

They were very happy to have helped Suma in any way they could, that's what friends are for.

***

Dylan Young
Age 9
Nottinghamshire, UK

"When they went back to Suma's house later to check how he was, they had taken him a cake that they baked together putting his favourite chocolate treat on top!"
– Dylan Young, Age 9

14. Ethan

ALWAYS BE KIND TO CHILDREN

When somebody, well most of the time, when somebody is hurt, I help them… a lot.

When I help them, they smile at me. When they smile at me, I smile at them. When they are crying, I say, "Are you ok?" and sometimes they say yes and sometimes they say nooooooo and are crying.

When they say no, I go and get help from a teacher.

I shout out loud to a teacher saying, "Please can you help this poor little child?". "OK", says the teacher who comes over and takes the child inside the classroom and they help them get better.

When I broke my wrist, everyone in my class was so nice to me, they helped look after me and signed my cast. I also got spotlight that week in assembly for being so positive and still working hard in school. When I had the cast removed, the nurses were so kind and helped cut the cast off with a special noisy, tickly tool. Then my wrist was ok, and I said thank you.

KINDNESS IS FREE FOR EVERYONE, SO BE KIND FOREVER!

***

Ethan Young
Age 6
Nottinghamshire, UK

15. Beth

The Kindness Kid

She has curly hair and beautiful blue eyes just like the bluey skies.

She always gives things to other people and has fun with her friends.

She is always kind to her friends and shares and plays nicely.

She says kind words and looks after people.

She loves animals and is kind to her cats.

She is very kind to her family and loves them very much.

She loves being kind to her sisters and always saves things for them.

***

Beth Dewhurst
Age 5
Lancashire, UK

16. Laura-Rose

The Kindness Superhero

The kindness hero flies all around the sky with her magical cape floating high.

She sprinkles her magical rainbow hero dust here, there and everywhere.

It slowly floats down and lands on people's heads and hands, allowing kindness to be spread around the world.

Where it lands, friends are made, and relationships are fresh and saved.

Hearts are filled with happiness and grow in kindness every day.

She flies around and makes a rainbow reminding people to be kind.

She makes her hero dust with love, happiness, joy, friendship and her secret ingredient, kindness.

The people it reaches learn how to be kind, generous, loving, patient, friendly and caring.

Watch out in the sky, you might just see her flying by.

Remember to always be friendly and kind to one another.

***

Laura Rose Dewhurst
Age 10
Lancashire, UK

17. Destiny

When you're walking down a street, what do you see? I see a beautiful white shop with mint-green additions, filled with alluring flowers. In front of the gaping door an old woman has fallen over. A lovely young woman is helping her up. She isn't kind, I know this as I watch the florist slip the older woman's purse into her back pocket.

I carry on walking down the street. I see a gentleman in slightly rugged clothing, completing his look with a large beanie on his head. His is walking my neighbour's mini-cockapoo and it's playing by his feet. He's not kind, I find this out as he lures another young pup out of number 42. By his worn-down shoes, I can tell he's taking them for the money.

I'm not kind. I watched the man take the dogs. I watched the florist put the woman's purse in her pocket. I did nothing. If I was kind, I would've told the lady to give the purse back and I would've made sure the dogs got back to their rightful owners. I turn around to make things right. I'm too late.

A young 13-year-old girl has yanked the purse out of the florist's pocket and given it back to the unknowing old-woman. She is kind. The owner of the dog about to be stolen has noticed and grabbed the leads of the two dogs and gotten them back. He is kind. We should all be kind.

***

Destiny Collings
Age 13
Devon, UK

18. Lexxi-Cameron

You can show kindness by reading with someone who doesn't understand something and appreciating a friend's success. You can show it, but you cannot wrap it up and give it to someone. Sometimes you can upset someone if you don't show kindness. A world without compassion and kindness could leave a hole in your heart. Kindness can lead to a warm smile. Kindness, generosity, and lots of it, can show that you respect someone. Kindness is not an emotion, it can and should be a common thing to give to someone. I show kindness all the time, not just by giving things to people but by putting other people's feelings before my own. I once gave my favourite doll to my little sister because she was upset. Kindness can be a simple thing like letting someone else go in front of you in a queue or helping someone feel safe if they look upset or lonely. When I am kind it gives me a warm, fuzzy and also proud feeling. If you are kind to someone, they may be kind to you or someone else and could eventually lead to the whole world being kind to each other.

***

Lexxi-Cameron Davis
Age 10
Devon, UK

19. Eden

The Dusty Room

Michael was an old man who was 94 years old. He lived on his own in a big house where he had lived with his family all his life. But now it was just him and he was lonely in the dusty room where he sat every day.

When he was young his legs could climb trees and run fast but now, they are bendy and wobbly, and he sits in a wheelchair. He cannot get out of the house as there are steps, he cannot climb, so he feels trapped like a prisoner.

Michael was feeling sad and upset when there was a knock at the door. It was a nurse. She wore white trousers, a blue top and a kind smile. "My name is Louise. I am here to help you."

They spoke about ways to make him feel better. She asked him, "How are you feeling?" No one had asked him this in such a long time, he enjoyed having someone to talk to and he began to feel more cheerful.

Louise looked at his legs, made him comfortable and got him some tea and toast. She spoke in a soft voice and her hands were very gentle, Michael felt much happier. More than any medicine she gave him, the kindness she showed him made him feel better.

Michael only began to feel sad when it was time for her to leave, but she told him, "I will come back tomorrow" and this made him smile as he sat alone again in the dusty room.

***

Eden Dine
Age 7
Copenhagen, Denmark

20. Grace

Kindness is my friends and family
They show love and care towards me
Kindness is when my friends and I play
When I feel sad they brighten up my day
Kindness is giving my little sister a teddy bear
Always showing her that I will be there
Kindness is helping someone in pain
Or sharing an umbrella under the rain
Kindness is looking after the old
And giving to the homeless out in the cold
Kindness is giving someone your seat
When I'm being kind, I feel it in my heartbeat.

***

Grace Francis-Mugurameno
Age 10
West Midlands, UK

21. Amber

Madam Kindness

Thousands of years ago, the sun watched over her world and didn't like what she saw. There was fighting, shouting and all the things she didn't want to see. The pure sadness of it all made her unable to shine.

So, she created a daughter and sent her down to the earth. She had no name. She smiled everywhere she went and laughed at any joke no matter how un-joke like it was. All of the other children said that she was 'weird and too good for her own good'. But the girl was kind to everyone no matter what they called her.

Then when she grew up, she decided to teach the new children about kindness. She got them in small groups and told them stories and gave lectures. They all loved her. She got the name of Madam Kindness.

She travelled around the world and gave everyone a chance to hear her stories, whether they were rich or poor. She did this for a living. She knew she could do more in her life, but her mother's people mattered more. Madam Kindness was only one of the billions of people her mother called her own.

Then one day, many years later, she passed away. All of the now grown up children were sad, but it wasn't the end of kindness. They told their children, who told theirs, making kindness something that has been passed down for generations and has shaped who we are today.

***

Amber McClintock
Age 10
Aberdeenshire, UK

22. Chloe

To me, kindness can be to anyone or anything. You can be kind to people like friends, family or just people in your community. However, you can also be kind to yourself by doing healthy things to your body like exercising or just as simple as eating nutritious food.

Furthermore, even though you don't think you are being kind to plants and nature when you water it and grow it, actually you are because you are helping it survive. So, your target for today is to be kind to as many people as you can.

***

Chloe Rose Wilson
Age 11
Nottinghamshire, UK

23. Kurt

Being Kind

When somebody helps me up, that is being kind.
When I have no one to play with and they play with me, that's being kind.
When somebody looks after me, that's being kind.
When somebody invites me to their party, that's being kind.
When somebody shares things with me, that's being kind.
When I am worried and somebody helps me to not be worried, that's being kind.
When somebody is being mean and somebody sticks up for me, that's being kind.
When somebody gives something to me, that's being kind.
When my mum cooks me something, that's being kind.
When I am kind, it makes me happy.

***

Kurt Mayle
Age 7
Nottinghamshire, UK

24. Callie

Kindness is, well, say I went out with my friend and I felt unhappy, they would try to cheer me up. They might say nice things to me or try to make me smile and laugh. KINDNESS is when someone has no money and you can give them some. KINDNESS is being polite to people, like holding doors open for people or helping them up if they have fallen over. Kindness is offering to share your sweets with your mummy or daddy, even though you really like the sweets. Kindness is making sure that you take good care of your pets by playing with them and stroking them and making sure they have food and water. Kindness means that sometimes you might have to do something that you don't really want to do. Kindness is showing people how much you love them; you could give them lots of hugs like I do with my Grandad. It is nice to be kind to people.

***

Callie Bland
Age 7
Leicestershire, UK

25. Mya

Kindness is:

- Not bullying people.

- If a friend is lonely in the school playground, go over to see if they would like to join in your game. This stops them from being sad and lonely.

- When one of your school friends returns from a music lesson, let them know what they need to do in class.

- Being nice to your friends and sharing your toys.

- Being helpful at school, like handing out books for the teacher.

- Saying thank you to anyone who holds the door open for you, and holding the door open for others.

- Using your manners all the time.

- Showing respect to teachers and other children.

- Being polite to everybody.

- Sending money to poor countries. This will help them to buy food and clothing.

- Helping raise money for charity.

- When one of your friends gets hurt, tell a teacher or help them.

- Picking up litter and keeping our planet clean and safe from pollution. This will keep all creatures safe.

- Putting up posters if a child or pet goes missing.

- Helping animals and insects when they are hurt - I saved a bee by giving it some sugary water when it was dehydrated during the summer.

- Treating animals with respect and not trying to harm them.

- Giving people compliments about how they look.

KINDNESS MAKES ME FEEL HAPPY AND IT MAKES THE WORLD A BETTER PLACE

***

Mya A
Age 8
Essex, UK

26. Finlay

Kindness is a very important thing to embrace throughout your lifetime.

Kindness is something everyone has, and you have it too.

It doesn't matter what age you are; you can always be kind. Kindness means accepting other people's differences. You are one in a million, you are you, only you can control you.

Kindness fills your heart with joy. If you do a good deed you will eventually benefit from it. You will not know when or how, but it will happen.

I am kind to people even if I am in a bad mood and when I feel angry. It does not feel good to be angry or mad all the time but sometimes you might wake up in a bad mood. If so, you should do something to change that because eventually, it causes stress in your body. You could become ill emotionally and physically. Kindness can change that; it makes me feel happy and it makes other people happy too.

The simplest kind deed you do can change the world in the biggest way. If you have thoughts about feeling good and want to make a difference in the world just be kind.

The movie 'Wonder' is about accepting the way some people are and not judging them by the way people might look and being kind. I love that movie. Being kind is a great way to live.

Remember always #kindiscool.

***

Finlay J. MacDonald
Age 10
Ottawa, Canada

27. Olivia

Kindness means that when people fall over, I will help them. When people are sad, I talk to them and let them play with me. You should be kind to everybody because it makes them happy, and when they are happy you are happy. Kindness is being nice to someone even if they are being mean to you. It's not always easy to be kind, sometimes I have to think about it, but I still decide to be kind because I'm a good person and I want people to be kind to me. My favourite way of being kind is letting people play with me. Another way to show kindness is by sharing the things you have with other people you love. You can also be kind by giving things to people that don't have as much as you, like food and clothes. The world would be better if everyone was kind as we would all be happy and helpful.

Olivia's Bio – I'm Olivia and I am 6 years old. I live with my mommy, daddy, brother, Henry and doggy, Pickle. I love making people laugh and smile. I like to colour and play games. My favourite movie is Captain Underpants and my favourite book is Wriggle and Roar!

***

Olivia Chambers
Age 6
Leicestershire, UK

"You can also be kind by giving things to people that don't have as much as you, like food and clothes. The world would be better if everyone was kind as we would all be happy and helpful." – Olivia Chambers, Age 6

28. Ruby

Sophia and the Crying Boy

One day, there lived a girl called Sophia. She went to the park and she saw someone crying. She asked them what the matter was. The boy didn't reply, and he kept on crying. Sophia said bye to the boy, and she gave him a big hug. The boy stopped crying. It was time for Sophia to go back home for her tea. Her mum gave Sophia her tea, she said, "Thank you Mum". She told her mum about the boy crying and she told her what she did. Her mum was very happy with her. The end.

***

Ruby Garbett
Age 7
West Midlands, UK

29. Aaron

What is kindness?

Kindness is sharing your chocolate
Giving my old toys to someone that doesn't have any
Not snatching stuff
Helping someone who is hurt, Giving them a band-aid
Giving Mummy her iPad back
Not calling people names
Saving someone who is being bullied
Making friends with someone who is all alone
Hugging Mummy when she is feeling poorly
Making popcorn for everyone
Patting Mummy's back when she is coughing

***

Aaron Chadwick
Age 9
Kent, UK

30. Seren

What does kindness mean to me?

Kindness means to care and to love.

It shows people that you are thinking of them.

Never give up on people.

Demonstrate that you respect them.

Never hurt or upset someone.

Enjoy helping friends and family, and spending time with them.

Support people when they need you.

Show someone that you accept them for who they are.

***

Seren
Age 7
Nottinghamshire, UK

31. Joshua

Kindness …

When your friend falls, help them up.

Help the homeless, a cup of coffee, a smile and one of your sweets.

When people are sad, help them forget about it, a hug, a story, do something nice.

Kindness is even just a smile. It's never JUST a smile.

***

Joshua James Cox Tunney
Age 9
Lanarkshire, UK

32. Georgia

Friendships

Kindness is about playing with your friends and making new friends and playing with them.

Kindness is about helping friends or other children when they are sad by giving them a big hug and asking if they would like to play with you, and also letting an adult know in case they can help too.

Kindness is about always speaking very kind words, especially when playing with my friends, as I don't want them to feel sad.

Kindness is about making cards and pictures for my friends, as I like my friends a lot.

Being kind is good as it makes people smile as well as making me smile.

***

Georgia Chester
Age 6
Nottinghamshire, UK

33. Oliver

Kindness

Kindness is snuggling up with Mummy and giving her hugs and kisses. With lots of love.

Is kindness what I think it is? Is it snuggling up with people and making them feel happy and loved? Yes, it is.

No one can be mean. Kindness should be the world.

Dare to be bad? You're stopped! Kindness is here!

Nothing can stop kindness; kindness is your passion.

Endless kindness, what a world that would be.

Something is pulling me, is kindness pulling you too?

Sadness should not rule the world. You know kindness is the best.

***

Oliver Haig
Age 7
Leicestershire, UK

34. Nathan

Kindness is like a superpower, it's such a good thing to master. If you ever need friends, then kindness is the go-to move.

In today's story, it's Ben that needs a friend.

One day (Tuesday, to be exact), Ben felt really lonely and sad. All he wanted was some friends to play Tig and Tag with. But Ben knew they would say no because last time he played, he cheated and saw where people hid and then he pushed someone.

Just when all hope for Ben to get some friends was lost, a huge muscular man appeared in the sunlight with a bright yellow cloak and a bold letter K for kind on his chest. It was Kindness Man!

He said to Ben, "I'm the superhero of kindness... Have you heard of kindness little boy?"

Ben looked at him confused and said, "No, what is it?"

"Well, it is the key to getting friends!"

Ben interrupted, "How do you know I want friends?"

Kindness Man replied with, "It's so obvious... You're alone and you look sad."

The superhero taught Ben how to be kind and caring. Now with Ben's new training, Ben is trying to make friends by sharing his toys and complimenting people.

Two weeks later he has lots of friends to play Tig and Tag with.

Just think this could be you. If you just use the power of kindness.

I hope you enjoyed my kindness story.

The End.

***

Nathan Phoenix Taylor
Age 10
Aberdeenshire, UK

35. Barney

Kindness makes the world the best place it could possibly be

Kindness is an easy thing to catch; it is like when you have the flu but better because kindness is a cheerful act of love.

It is beneficial to others who receive and generously share kindness, it makes the world a better place, we could all do with more kindness each day.

Noble is a person who gives to others such as the homeless. Especially when they have little to give themselves, they are super kind!

Decent people are the people who are loving and likable to others because of their outstanding kindness towards other people.

Nice qualities of people who are kind are: pleasant, happy, sweet, generous, thoughtful, positive and willing to share the love.

Easy-going acts of kindness are being a good listener, giving compliments, smiling, offering your help to others and holding a door for someone.

Smiling is infectious because it makes people feel recognised and loved. So, if you see someone without their smile, share your kindness with them because it doesn't hurt or cost anything.

So just be kind, it's as simple as that!

These are my ideas about kindness, follow them and you may spread that kindness around the world. Start at home and it will spread with each person who passes it on.

***

Barney Ainsworth
Age 10
Manchester, UK

36. Severn

Here are lots of ways that you can show kindness!

If one of your friends is upset or if they have no one to play with, a kind person would go up to them and ask them to play with them, so they aren't on their own.

Giving things to homeless people is kind especially if you give them warm food. I like to give homeless people warm food and buy them a Costa so it can keep their hands and insides warm.

If someone needs help, like if there was an animal that was dying near a road and no one knew the number for the ambulance, then I would go and call an ambulance for them.

If there's someone new at school and they don't know anyone and if they're from a different country, you make them feel welcome as if they were back in their old normal school so that they feel ok.

If there's someone who's happy and fine or sad and down but you are just in a good mood, you can compliment anyone to just make them feel good as well that day.

In my school, we give Tzedakah every Wednesday which

is where we give money to a charity and I think that's really kind because the money goes to help lots of people.

I won the headteachers monthly megastar award at school for showing kindness to everyone and I felt really proud!

I like being kind.

***

Severn Seymour
Age 7
Manchester, UK

37. Dexter

Kindness

Kindness is love, it means helping people, like helping people up when they fall over or helping people walk if they find it hard. It also means sharing, like sharing a toy or sharing snacks with someone when they don't have any and you do.

Kindness means giving other people things that they need, like when you get too big for your clothes and shoes and you give them away so other people can have them. I think kindness is standing up for someone if other people are being mean or inviting someone to play if they're alone.
Kindness is giving someone a hug or making them laugh if they are sad, it means listening to them and telling people you love them.

The world needs more kindness, stopping bullying and stopping cutting the rainforest down for the animals. We need to be kind to them. Everyone needs kindness, it makes you smile and your heart happy.

***

Dexter Harry Woodward
Age 7
Lancashire, UK

38. Kyle

When I wake up in the morning, I ask my family if they had a lovely sleep and give them a big cuddle. I do that to be kind.

When I leave to go to school, I tell my mum to have a nice day. I do that to be kind.

When I am at school, I will tell someone a joke if they look sad. I do that to be kind.

When I play with my toys, I like to share with my friends. I do that to be kind.

When I do my work in class, I always help others if they don't know what to do. I do that to be kind.

When I have my lunch, I say thank you to the dinner lady for cooking my food. I do that to be kind.

When I am in the playground and one of my friends falls over, I always help them up. I do that to be kind.

When I am at the childminders I help to look after the younger children. I do that to be kind.

When I get home in the evening, I tell my family I missed them today. I do that to be kind.

When I go to bed and snuggle my teddy, I tell my family I love them. I do that to be kind.

And the most important question to ask myself before falling asleep is…was I kind to myself today? I do that to be kind.

***

Kyle Stevenson
Age 5
Cheshire, UK

39. Sienna

Kindness is doing nice things, sharing the love towards those who you see are struggling, even considering animals or the planet like with the bushfires, providing water to wild animals by leaving containers of water out and donating stuff to those who have lost everything.

I like cutting a flower and giving it to someone, and watching the happiness on their face… That's kindness.

I think that by going around and doing nice things it makes people feel good and makes me feel good too, so it helps you be a better person and makes our world a better place.

If everyone could do one act of kindness each day, even the smallest thing, we could make the world a happier place to live in, so everyone could have peace and no war. It would be nice to see more positive vibes from everyone around the world, I think it's needed.

There are so many things, big and small, that people can do to show kindness. I have listed 8 here that I would like to share with you:

Keep being kind and spread happy vibes
If someone is down help them be happy
Nothing is better than making someone smile
Don't hurt people or our planet
No bullying each other, just spread love
Everyone is different so show respect and accept people
for who they are
Saying thank you and showing manners
So, choose kindness!

***

Sienna Ngeru
Age 8
Sydney, Australia

40. Olivia

Kindness is important.
In the world, there are some not very nice people; you should always try to be kind.
No-one should be treated badly and made to feel sad.
Don't be mean, be kind! It's simple!
Never treat people a way you would not like to be treated.
Everyone deserves to be happy,
So, we should always try to be kind.
Smile at other people, make them smile too.

***

Olivia Bartram
Age 9
England, UK

41. Charlotte

Kindness is…
…the helping of hands for friends.
…Mummy and Daddy helping me with homework.
…helping my sisters tidy up.
…playing with people who have been left out.
…having kind hands and feet.
…not shouting or saying something mean to friends or family.
…picking up somebody if they fall over.
…helping your mummy and daddy do the washing up or washing.
…not leaving people out.
…saying "sorry" if you accidently push or say something mean to your friends or family.
…to make somebody feel welcome if they are new.
…to listen to your friends and family.
…saying "thank you" to people if they give you something.
…looking after your pets.

Kindness is simple acts to make a day better for someone.
I wonder what your kindness is?

***

Charlotte Spiby
Age 8
West Midlands, UK

42. Alice

Tips for Being Kind by Alice

Make sure somebody has a friend if they are lonely or upset.
Make people happy and not sad.
Smile, it might brighten someone's day.
Being silly can be fun but not when it makes someone else sad.
Be kind to people.
If someone is being horrible, ask them to stop.
Stick up for your friends.
Be a friend to everyone.
Hold a door or gate open for the next person.
Never do things that someone says no to.
Read someone a story.
Be the best friend you can be.
Be a listening ear, when people are talking to you.
Be nice and friendly.
Help other people.
Be helpful to friends who are stuck with their work.
Enjoy time with grandparents, they have lots of fun things to teach us.
Welcome new people and make them feel at home.
Help your family by doing little chores like watering the plants.

And don't forget…
Be kind to yourself!

***

Alice Spiby
Age 6
West Midlands, UK

43. Sahm

When I was almost four, I tripped, and I fell over. My knee got big and really sore and I had to go to hospital. I was rushed to surgery because I had septic arthritis, I think that is how you say it? My surgeon was great, he helped me to fall asleep so he could make me better. I didn't like staying in the hospital, but my friends came and gave me gifts and when I felt really bad my Dad would tell me jokes. This was how they showed their kindness to me. The doctors did everything they could to help me go home. They kept coming into my room, a lot. Because of them I didn't have to stay for years and years, just weeks and weeks. I was ok until this year when I felt really bad again. A doctor in a big white room with a big smile told my mum and dad that I have an illness that won't go. I was worried a lot. My mum cried. My brothers have the illness too. But I feel positive because all the doctors and nurses we see are super kind! They make me feel brave when I have to get medicines in my arm. They really hurt. Now, I need to be extra kind to my younger brother, like my older brother is to me, he is really afraid of needles and if I encourage him and be strong it means he won't be sad. Being kind is really important!

***

Sahm Henry
Age 7

"I didn't like staying in the hospital, but my friends came and gave me gifts and when I felt really bad my Dad would tell me jokes. This was how they showed their kindness to me." – Sahm Henry, Age 7

44. Layla

Kindness

Kindness is about helping others, it's about sharing, letting others do things you don't want to do but you still do it anyway because you love them. Here are a few of the kind things I do.

Sharing

I share things like my wigs, my old phone and puzzles. I share my wigs with my sister, my puzzles with Theodore and my old phone with my youngest brother. Sometimes I share my sweets with them too.

Helping

I help people by doing things to help them, I pick up things if people drop them, I help people figure things out when they can't decide and sometimes I try to behave so I can stop annoying people.

Compliments

Telling people they look nice, saying their hair is nice, saying that they smell nice, telling them their eyes are pretty, telling them their clothes/dress/top/trousers are nice, that they have a nice personality and telling them that they're beautiful, no matter what, are all acts of kindness.

Doing stuff you don't want to do but you still do it for them

I let people choose what to do even if I don't like it, I let Alicia keep my phone when she steals it, I let people watch things I don't like on TV, I go to places even if I don't want to go there, I do photoshoots with Alicia even if I don't want to and sometimes I play with my brothers, although they can be annoying.

***

Layla Novelli
Age 10
Surrey, UK

45. Theo

My top five kindness things to do.

There are many ways to show your kindness, here are a few of my favourite ways:

I like to share my Nintendo Switch, my favourite electronic, with Layla and Toby, my sister and brother, because I love to see them happy and it makes my heart drop.

Sometimes someone gets sad, I show my kindness by giving them a nice hug. They get happy because they know I care.

I like to be kind for my mum by tidying my toys, being good and always using my manners. It is sometimes hard to do these things but when I do, it makes both me and Mummy happy.

At the park, if I see someone with no one to play with, I will play with them because being kind makes me feel happy, and it makes them happy too.

Sometimes I even share my last sweet with my brother or sister because it makes us all happy.

Kindness is so important, and everyone should be kind,

even if only one time a day because it makes the world a happy place.

Who will you be kind to today?

***

Theodore Novelli
Age 7
Surrey, UK

46. Arianna

Hello everyone! I am Arianna and I am 7yrs old and I live in England with my mummy, daddy, my dog called Maggie, a cat and chameleon!

3 years ago, two kind ladies called Lesley and Laura found a dog called Maggie.
She lived on the streets, she was cold, lonely and hungry.
Maggie could only eat from bins.
Maggie was put on the happy plane to fly to England to find her new forever family!

By the time she got there it was Valentine's Day and she ended up in London, which is a very big city, with lots of people.

Maggie was lost and hungry, suddenly she saw a homeless lady who gave her some of her food and let her sleep on her cosy blanket. The lady was very kind to Maggie.

So, even if you only have a little bit to give, you can still be kind.

After a long walk from London to Camberley, Maggie walked up a long street which had lots of lovely houses on it.

Then she saw a little girl with blonde hair. The girl was stroking a big fluffy ginger cat. The cat looked very happy and the little girl was kind to the cat.

Maggie decided she wanted to live in that house too!

Maggie barked outside the house and the little girl came out to see her.

Maggie chased the big ginger cat and the little girl thought she was funny, so she let her into the house.

Now Maggie is happy in her new home with her new family and an annoying big ginger cat!

***

Arianna Storrs-Barbor
Age 7
Surrey, UK

47. Annabel

Kindness to me is helping someone when they are down.
It is a power of magic.
Never be unkind.
Do your best to help others.
Never say mean words.
Every day show respect to everyone.
Say nice things to cheer people up.
Share with everyone.

***

Annabel Sophia Wilkins
Age 6
Derbyshire, UK

48. Khwaish

"Please welcome the new girl, Layla," the teacher said smiling. Shyly, Layla smiled from the front of the class. She felt embarrassed as she did not like being the centre of attention.

Melanie shrieked, "Look what she's wearing!"

Layla glanced down at her outfit. She had spent ages choosing it the night before, eager for her first day. But now she felt awkward in it. She could see the contrast against everyone else's.

Layla felt like she could burst into tears. She was looking forward to today, her first day and it was already a disaster, even though it had just started. Looking at her feet, she maneuvered towards the only chair in the room, next to a snickering boy and a girl, who was smiling at her affectionately.

"I like your clothes," the girl declared, "I'm Luciana but you can call me Lucy."

Immediately, Layla felt better, as she could feel the warmth emitting from this girl.

At playtime, the mean girl, Melanie, came over. "Come on, Luce."

"You go ahead. I'm going to play with Layla." Luciana said bravely.

Melanie looked at her friend scornfully, "Why would you want to play with her?"

"Because she's nice. Nicer than you at least."

"Fine," Melanie sneered, "I'll just go play with Clementine."

For once, Luciana didn't feel sad. She felt good. She had helped someone. She had been kind to someone. Unlike the rest of the class, who had just sat and watched and laughed.

***

Khwaish Amarnani
Age 13
Panama

49. Lennie

Once upon a time, there was a chicken called Clown. He was nothing like a clown. All he wanted was a friend.

Clown had 'friends' (which were not real friends). There was a duck called Pom who had no friends either.

"Hi Clown", whispered Pom.

"H-hi Pom, w-want to have a play day?" replied Clown.

"Ok, where?" said Pom.

"My house?" said Clown.

"S-sure", replied Pom.

Later that day, Pom and Clown were walking home, and a UFO abducted them. Clown looked up and saw an alien. The alien took off his helmet and… he was a human! He explained that no one liked him either. He hid away from society. He had green skin, and everyone thought he was a freak.

Pom and Clown told him about how no one liked them either. They only had each other. The human was called Ian. Ian explained how he could take them around the universe and explore.

They went around the universe going to lots of planets visiting aliens. After years of going around the universe they flew into the sun and… lived!

They had no one to bother them or bully them; they would never leave.

Until one day a turtle called Pow flew to the sun and told them to go back to Earth because it was a different place.

Everyone was friendly and kind; not one mean person. They all lived happily ever after.

***

Lennie Farren
Age 11
Northamptonshire, UK

50. Daisy

A Recipe for a Kind Person

1. 1 cup of kindness sugar
2. 1 drop of helpfulness
3. 2 teaspoons of cuddles
4. ½ cup of thoughtfulness
5. 3 cups of patience

Stir it up together then add a tablespoon of love

AND THAT'S HOW YOU MAKE A KIND PERSON!

***

Daisy Nurse
Age 7
Leicestershire, UK

51. Abby

To be loving and caring is important to me,
Being a good friend, the best I can be,
When a friend is in need, I help their needs to be met,
They might be quiet and not want to talk yet.

Friends might have problems they don't want to share,
But being a kind friend, letting them know I care,
Time is more precious and all that it's worth,
Is much more important than things bought on this Earth.

Kindness comes from within,
If you can help, you can win,
Giving is receiving, a smile on a face,
Start off slow then build at a pace.

You'll always have someone by your side,
Whether they are close by or across the tide,
Even if your loved ones are far apart,
Kindness can touch someone's heart.

***

Abby Brown
Age 11
Leicestershire, UK

52. Tane

Kindness is my superpower and it's a special thing in life too. Kindness helps you to have the ability to make friends. I'll tell you how I became friends with my best friend. We didn't used to get on and we didn't used to be friends but over the months, I learnt something about kindness, I saw something good in his heart that made me become friends with him and through our time at school, he cared about me and supported me and I did the same to him.

Kindness is about being thoughtful, loving, caring and honest to those around us. To be kind often takes courage and strength, bullies try to find our weaknesses, using it to annoy us, to hurt us and to get us in to trouble. We shouldn't allow bullies to take our kindness but to teach them kindness.

***

Tane Brown
Age 9
Leicestershire, UK

53. Nykera

Kindness Starts with You

Kindness always starts within. Be kind to yourself then be kind to others. Kindness is more than just a compliment or a hug, it's being generous and grateful, not just to others but to yourself also. How are you kind to yourself?

Do you take a nap? Have a relaxing bubble bath? Eat your favourite snack? Whatever you do, kindness always starts with you.

It makes a person feel awesome when they get a compliment. How do you feel when you get a compliment? Proud? Confident? Happy?

Kindness isn't something you're born with, it is something you learn. Kindness can come in any shape or form. Even if you do the smallest thing or the most amazing thing for someone, it's still an act of kindness, which is why we should all be kind and spread love.

I love spreading kindness; it makes me feel so happy to see a smile on someone's face.

To me, kindness is spreading love and getting rid of the

hate. In this world there is so much hate so we all should be lifting each other up.

Being kind has so many different definitions, but it always starts with you.

In a world full of hate choose kindness; you never know the affect it can have on someone. It could change their whole mindset.

Always stay positive because that's what kindness is all about.

Whatever you do kindness starts with you.

***

Nykera Kelly
Age 12
Derbyshire, UK

54. Sophie

I think kindness means being thoughtful, caring, sharing and being helpful.

If someone fell over, it would be kind to help them up.

If someone had no one to play with, it would be kind to invite them to play with you and make new friends.

When you invite family and friends around to your house and if cousins are being too rough to your friends then you can kindly suggest that they play a better game together that you all like.

One of my friends at school is kind because when we were on the tyres, I was waiting for someone to jump to another tyre and someone behind me was waiting for me to move on and I said, "Wait until the person in front of me has jumped to another tyre", but he didn't, and he pushed me off. My friend was very kind, she looked after me and took me to a teacher.

In class, if you were creating something and someone ran out of something, it is kind to share your materials and tools with them.

If someone is sad, it is kind to try and cheer them up.

If your parents were looking for something and they couldn't find it, you could try to get it for them for Christmas or their birthday.
My mummy was kind as she helped me to do this project.

***

Sophie Crook
Age 8
Staffordshire, UK

55. Molly

This is what kindness is to me:

K indness makes me happy,
I ncluding people is
N ice and caring,
D elighted friends because of you,
N ot making people sad,
E njoyable times come from kindness,
S haring good times with friends to make them happy,
S o, these are all random acts of kindness.

***

Molly Grace Banks
Age 10
Derbyshire, UK

56. Sophie

This is what Kindness means to me…

Show **Grace**
Always have **Faith** in you
Be kind to **Friends**
Give **Warm** hugs like Olaf
Always **Love** others
Always **Share** toys
Always **Care** when people fall over
Show your **Feelings**
Always **Hope** stuff will go right
Always be **Unselfish**

***

Sophie Faith Banks
Age 6
Derbyshire, UK

57. Ellie

The Kindness of Arnie

Before I start this story, I would like to tell you that this it is about my friend, Arnie.

Once, me and Arnie went to the park for a walk together; we go every day. One strange day we went down to the park and when we got halfway through our walk, Arnie ran off! So, obviously I chased him and called him, and he just kept running! Eventually, he stopped and pointed at a little boy in a ditch. We asked the boy what had happened, so he told us everything. I pulled him out of the ditch, and we went to go find the boy's friends and tell them what had happened. When we were looking for the little boy's friends, he told us how long he had been in there, and he had been in there for 30 minutes. He also said he was very happy that we had saved him. When we did find his friends, they all wondered where he had been, and they were very happy that we helped him too.

THE END…

P.S. This is not a real story and Arnie was a dog, his breed was a black Labrador Retriever.

Arnie got really excited whenever he met new people! He was kind and loved playing around with everyone.

Kindness is my friends when I feel sad.

Kindness is my Mum and Dad!

I know people care.

Everyone should share.

Everyone can be kind.

To everyone they find.

R.I.P
Arnie

***

Ellie Rose Clements
Age 9
Nottinghamshire, UK

58. Jack

Alfie and The Lonely Dinosaur

Alfie loves going on adventures with his time travelling watch.

His watch is magical, and he's seen many amazing things on his travels.

One day Alfie woke up

Suddenly, out the corner of Alfie's eye he saw a giant egg!!! He ran towards the entrance of the cave. Out of nowhere, a huge boulder fell down and covered the entrance of the cave! It was pitch black.

Alfie's watch also has a torch, which he used to shine light in the cave.

Alfie wandered to the darkest part of the cave and saw the egg had hatched. He stumbled backwards and bumped into a baby dinosaur.

Alfie wasn't afraid because Dino looked very lonely and sad. His mum was nowhere to be seen. Alfie felt sorry for him and decided to look after Dino. They played hide and seek, tag, monsters and then they had a little nap.

When they woke up, they realised Dino's mum had managed to move the boulder away. She was so happy to see Dino had hatched and was grateful to Alfie for looking after her baby while they were stuck.

Soon it was time for Alfie to go home. Dino's mum thanked him for being so kind and she named Dino after his new friend.

Alfie went home to bed and looked forward to his next adventure.

***

Jack Pierce
Age 7
Berkshire, UK

"Alfie wandered to the darkest part of the cave and saw the egg had hatched. He stumbled backwards and bumped into a baby dinosaur." – Jack Pierce, Age 7

59. Harry

Sebastian's Cake

Hi, my name is Sebastian. I'm a raccoon, but I'm not like the rest of the raccoons round here. They're all trying to get their next dinner by going into the human's houses and raiding their white cold boxes without asking. I want to do something kind for the humans. I'm gonna make them a cake.

For the ingredients I need:

4 flowers
1 rainbow
3 pieces of paper
A paw full of sugar

There we go! Now time to get them!

I went to Mr Smiley's house and I picked some flowers, I got some sugar packets from the forest cafe, and some paper from a dustbin by the school. Now I need to get a rainbow! I saw one behind the mountain, so I ran to get it. When I got there, it seemed like it moved but it was still there and it was further away, so I did the best and only thing any raccoon could do.

I asked my butterfly friends if they could help me catch the rainbow. After a while, they finally caught it! I thanked the butterflies and got all I needed and started to mix.

It was finished! Finally!

I gave the cake to Mr Smiley; he was really kind and grateful and guess what! I got a home! It's really nice and comfortable and I think I'm gonna be kind more often.

***

Harry Mack
Age 11
Essex, UK

60. Lilly

Kindness is about friendship and not being unkind.
Kindness is sharing, not bullying.

Bullying is saying mean things and doing unkind things. It's not nice to be a bully and you should tell a teacher if someone is bullying you at school.

Kindness is about having good friends and making sure they aren't being bullied and don't bully other people.

It is kind to share everything you want to.

If you are crying in a corner, go and tell a teacher, parent or friend.

If you fall over, people will come up to you and help you; kindness is just about helping each other.

It is kind to help tidy stuff or walk the dog.

Be kind, not mean to each other; we are all friends.

My Great-Grandad is poorly, we are kind to him and love him very much.

Gracie is kind to me when she cuddles me in the playground.

I am kind to my granny when I help her make pizza.

I am kind to my dog, Milo, I play with him and give him treats.

It feels nice when people are kind to me.

I am kind to my friends when I play a game they want me to, but I don't really want to.

Always be kind.

***

Lilly Cecelia Connon
Age 8
Nottinghamshire, UK

61. Max

Kindness is friendship, happiness and joy,
You can offer a smile or buy someone a toy.
If worse comes to worst, family always comes first,
You can make someone happy without opening your purse!

Kindness really is the best,
If you don't believe me, please put it to the test.
Kindness is fun and so easy to share,
Kindness is the best way of showing that you care.

Buy some flowers, open a door or make a cup of tea,
Kindness is for everyone and is as easy as 1, 2, 3!

***

Max Barrett-Myler
Age 13
UK

62. Jack

Kindness is fun
Be nice to your mum.

It's important to be kind
It's good for your mind.

Kindness is cool
Be kind at home and school.

Make someone smile
It will make them happy for a while.

Kindness is fun. It really is.
The kindest person I know is my Aunty Liz.

I try to be kind each and every day
As it makes me happy in every single way!

***

Jack Barrett-Myler
Age 9
UK

63. Jax

Kindness means to me, being nice, sharing, greeting other people, giving cards and presents on things like Valentine's Day, for example, and Christmas and birthdays and Easter and Halloween.

It's having good relationships, not bullying people.

It's looking after the planet, saving people from dying, maybe.

Kindness is also about raising money for charity and that is what kindness means to me.

Bye!

***

Jax Strasdin
Age 8
Carmarthenshire, UK

64. Erika

Helping

Being kind is who I am. When my little sister is sick, I take her a blanket and snuggle her in. I like looking after her to make her feel better but also to help my mummy. Helping people shows that you are kind.

Sharing

When I have sweeties, I share with my friends. I also share with my brother even though he never shares with me. Mummy says it makes me the better person. It feels nice to share because not everybody has what I have. Seeing other people happy makes me feel good.

Caring

Sometimes people are having a really bad time and they won't tell you. It's important to always be nice to other people because you just don't know how sad they are feeling. Being kind to everybody could make one person feel happy again.

Mummy says that if you can be anything in this life, be kind.

***

Erika-Karen Jordan
Age 8
Obertraun, Austria

65. Alicia-Mae

The dictionary defines kindness as being "…generous, kind and considerate to others".

To me kindness is simply thinking of others. My family isn't rich, we don't have a lot, but I have a roof over my head, food and water in my stomach, and a loving, caring family.

I am lucky, I am happy, but not everyone is as lucky as I am.

My sister and I wanted to pay it forward so a year ago we started a small business making wish bracelets, to raise money for those who may be less fortunate than us and in helping others it in turn makes me feel contented knowing that I may have helped to spread a little kindness.

Most people think that kindness takes energy, time and resources but kindness doesn't have to be a big gesture; it could be as simple as talking to someone if they look lonely or upset or complimenting them on their glasses, outfit or new haircut. Small gestures like this can create a ripple of kindness and can have a huge effect on the rest of their day.

We don't know the battles people are facing but sometimes the nicest thing we can do is just be kind.

Kindness is infectious and needs to be spread all over the world, so make someone happy today, smile at them, share a compliment or two and do something that will help someone feel important and valued.

Let kindness be included in the template of your day and let's work together to make the world a kinder place.

***

Alicia-Mae Grimshaw Bonsu
Age 11
Staffordshire, UK

66. Olivia

What Kindness Means to Me

I sat down with my grand-dad Paul, and we talked about kindness and what it means to me…

Kindness means that we all respect each other and are nice to one another. Kindness means treating people how you would like to be treated yourself – that's kindness.

I like to help people, if they fall over or hurt themselves, or if they are in a wheelchair and need help to get around.

At school I always help people, like my friends, to finish their work and always be polite to teachers and staff.

Even if other children are not one of my friends, I always try and play with them, if they seem lonely.

It makes me feel happy, when people are kind to me, and I am kind to them…

***

Olivia Jasmine Boaler
Age 7
Nottinghamshire, UK

67. Shantul

Kindness Wins the Day

Once upon a time, there lived two little girls who were not very good friends. In fact, they were not friends at ALL! At school, Arya would make rude faces at Shantul, then Shantul would make rude faces back at Arya.

One day, at school, they were chosen to put the register away TOGETHER! They started to argue about who was going to hold the register, but they wasted so much time squabbling that a teacher caught them. They were told to write a story project on kindness, but they had to do it TOGETHER.

They were not happy and started to write furiously about all the things they hated about each other. Slowly, they looked at each other and found their cross faces quite funny. They started to giggle, laugh even! They started to write again. This time, they wrote about good memories between them. There had been some good times! They had forgotten. Ever since that day, they try to remember the good things about each other when they have a fall out. That is the kind thing to do, especially when you are best friends.

***

Shantul
Age 6
Bedfordshire, UK

68. Michael

Kindness to me is helping others when they need it…

Once upon a time, on an undiscovered planet called ##Earth there was a red and blue alien called ##Rel. One day he saw a poor little donkey (known as a ##Donkey!) in a tree and so ##Rel called "ddd" (that's like 999 on ##Earth) and told the fire station. The donkey was only the size of a cat (as ##donkeys tend to be). ##Rel saw an old ladder and he climbed up the ladder but couldn't reach the donkey. Suddenly the fire brigade came and passed him up another ladder to get to the poor donkey. ##Rel got the donkey and the donkey licked him to say thanks…

Once down from the tree ##Rel fell into a pit and only the donkey saw. ##Rel thought, 'no way is a donkey going to save me, I'm going to be stuck for a long, long time'. But he was wrong. The donkey ran to the fire brigade and dragged a fireman's coat to where ##Rel had fallen. Once ##Rel was out of the pit, he and the donkey became best friends forever.

So, if you're kind to someone they will be kind back.

***

Michael Čolan
Age 10
Leicestershire, UK

69. Blake

What kindness means to me.

Being kind makes me happy. My kindness makes other people happy and makes them smile. If you are unkind to people, it will make everyone upset.

You can be kind to someone like saying, "Your shirt is nice."

I have kind friends. We all look after each other and play nicely.

My brother Michael is also very kind to me. He makes sure that I am feeling OK and having fun. So, kindness makes other people very happy. Being nice and kind makes everyone happy.

I am kind because I help my friends a lot.

***

Blake Čolan
Age 7
Leicestershire, UK

70. Lily

Kindness and Friendship Matters

If you're lonely, you make a friend. And then you've got some friendship forever. Where your friendship lasts forever, you will live there. And your friend will too. You can make some more friends to make some more friendship between everyone. Kindness comes from a smile. And love. And family; your mummy and daddy. Kindness comes from inside your heart.

And you've got your teddy if you feel lonely. If you are alone, you say, "Please can I play, and please may I be your friend?" and that's how you make friendship. You have to be kind to your friend. You take turns, you play fair.

If you've got a pet, you stroke it a lot and if your friend comes around, it's their turn to stroke it. If you're doing a pretend tea party, the cake has to be split fairly so you and your friend won't argue. You can make friendship bracelets and a friendship book. You've got kindness all around. You know because everyone says, "Please may I play?" Pleases and thank yous make friends too.

If you've got a favourite tv show, you have to share it with your friends and share everything, even your teddy. Sometimes you have to play what your friend wants to play even though you don't want to. That's being kind.

***

Lily Cailey
Age 6
UK

71. Tilly

Interview with Tilly about what kindness is to her

Mum: "Tilly, let's talk about kindness. What is being kind?"

Tilly: "Hugs, kisses, playing, cleaning up…"

Mum: "Ooohh that's nice, if you saw someone at the park and they were upset what kind of things could you do to make them happy?"

Tilly: "Get them a plaster."

Mum: "That's kind, isn't it? If someone is sad, what could you do to make them happy that's kind?"

Tilly: "A kiss, hugs, and go home, go to doctors, flowers…"

Mum: "What else is kind?"

Tilly: "Wait, Jacob gave me a cake, that's kind, yeah? Guess what Mum, flowers are kind too."

Mum: "In school, who is kind?"

Tilly: "Russell, yeah, Russell is kind. Jacob is my friend."

Mum: "What kind things does Russell do in school?"

Tilly: "Playing, sitting next to me, I get sad when no one sits next to me, but Russell sits next to me."

Mum: "Is that kind, do you think?"

Tilly: "Yeah, that's kind. Russell is kind, Jacob said, 'I will sit next to Tilly too'."

Mum: "That's very kind, isn't it? If Grandma was sad, what kind things could make her happy?"

Tilly: "Flowers, ermmm watching tv, going to the doctors, putting a blanket on her, get her water and medicine..."

Mum: "That's so nice, Tilly. Is it good to be kind?"

Tilly: "Yeah, I'm kind Mum."

Mum: "Who are all the kind people you know?"

Tilly: "Elsa, Sian, Grandma, me, baby Violet, and erm Violet is still small but when it's Christmas she was tiny and kind, I play with her, yeah she laughs at me. I give her cuddles, that's kind, isn't it?"

Mum: "It certainly is Tilly; you are a very kind little girl."

***

Tilly Auger
Age 4
Merseyside, UK

72. Marcus

It was a Monday morning; Joe woke up and went downstairs to eat his lovely white chocolate Coco Pops, when he realised that there were none left. He groaned and reluctantly went outside into town, to get his Coco Pops from the supermarket. When he got to the cereal aisle, he saw that there were none left. Joe groaned as he picked up the normal Coco Pops and stormed out of the shop.

On his way home, he walked past a boy who was around 12 years old. He was poor and starving. Joe just looked at him and said, "You need to go win the lottery or something. Stop expecting people to give you anything." The boy realised that when Joe was a little boy, he had nothing too, abandoned on the streets, starving, poor and nobody gave him money or food. That night, the boy found some paper on the floor and started to write a long letter to Joe asking him to reflect on his actions.

The next morning, he rang the doorbell of Joe's house and posted the letter. When Joe woke up, he went downstairs and saw the letter, so he read it. He instantly started thinking about when he was younger, when he had nothing, and he realised he wanted the boy to have a better life than he did.

So, with the letter in hand, Joe went out seeking for the boy. He finally found him and said, "Why don't you come live with me, there's plenty of room for you." Joe and the child lived happily ever after.

***

Marcus Auwkit
Age 11
Nottinghamshire, UK

73. Bess

Kindness is needed
In the world
Never stop spreading love
Do the right thing
Never stop believing
Even if it's hard
Seek kindness in people
See kindness in yourself

Friends have a special bond
Real friends trust and appreciate each other
It doesn't matter where you are
Even if you are miles apart
Never break this special bond
Don't be scared to speak your heart

***

Bess Moseley
Age 11
Kent, UK

74. Harry

Kindness at Golden Sands

Kindness was when a friendly adult gave my mummy their tickets that they had won on the machines for me to keep. Mummy said, "Thank you", and I did too.

Kindness was when I picked up a lady's walking stick that had fallen onto the floor to give it back to her. She smiled and said "Thank you" which was also kind. Then, my daddy bought me and Georgia some sweets for being kind.

Kindness is when another kind adult gave me and Georgia their left-over tokens for the fair as it was their last day and they saw me waiting to go on the ride. I said "Thank you" because they were kind.

Kindness was when Georgia gave me some of her coins to play on the machines as mine had ran out. I said "Thank you" to Georgia and gave her a big hug for being kind.
I like being kind.

***

Harry Chester
Age 4
Nottinghamshire, UK

75. Iman

The Light Face of Kindness

Splat! Raspberry ripple,
Oozing out over the dusty concrete,
Topped with a corn cone hat.
Out of all the smirking faces
Comes one with a concerned smile.
Behold! An upright cone with a creamy dollop! How's that?!

Brrrrr! Fingers blue from the cold.
Sleeping bag torn, "S-s-spare s-some ch-change?"
Shoes and clothes all worn.
Out of all the turning away faces
Comes one that doesn't flinch,
Warming the heart inch by inch.

Gone! A love has gone!
Grief like lead; can't get out of bed.
Can't get a straight heart, hand or head.
Out of all the awkward faces
Comes one with hope and feeling tears.
All is not as lost as it appears.

Kindness has many a face,
Picks the best one for the place.
It's not as hard as it seems;
Don't be one of the faceless,
Lightless. Be the one that
Beams.

***

Iman
Age 10
Bedfordshire, UK

76. Charlotte

To me kindness means being caring and being kind to others. It also means being thoughtful, loving, helpful and even considerate.

What you can do to be KIND:

You can help others if they are upset or hurt. The other ways of being kind are being respectful and saying nice things to make people feel better.

People you can be kind TO:

EVERYONE; Like your mum or your dad or your family. You can also smile to people you don't know on the streets. Because it is a kind thing to do.

Examples of being KIND:

I helped my nan tidy the house.
I helped a homeless person.
I was kind to my friend by saying a good comment like, "Your dress is beautiful".

***

Charlotte Holly Pascoe
Age 9
Essex, UK

77. Madison

Kindness to an Aussie 6yr old is...

Kindness is respecting and helping others, even when they don't ask you to. It's not nice to let anyone be lonely, or hungry, or sad. You always have to help someone that you see that might be hurt or needs some help.

Kindness is sharing my toys with my cousin Jayden, when he has nothing else to play with. We take turns playing games. I don't mind playing games that he wants to play first. Then I get to choose what game to play next.

I was very sick in hospital, and all the doctors and nurses were very kind when they were looking after me. I want to be a nurse when I grow up, so I can be kind and help other sick people get better. My entire Kindy class wrote me some get well soon cards, and my best friends came to visit me in hospital and bought me presents and games to play. I was so excited and love them very much. That was very kind of them.

Kindness is looking after my two pet kittens and playing with them to keep them happy and healthy, and cleaning up my mess around the house, so nobody trips over.

I like to be kind and helpful to my friends and teachers at school. My teacher Mr Wade is very helpful and kind to all of us. He makes us all laugh, and I love going to my school.

***

Madison Rose Sillett
Age 6
NSW, Australia

78. Zakiyya

Kindness

One winter Saturday, Agnes Parker was taking a stroll to the park when she noticed a sharp pin laying on the floor, it immediately screamed 'DANGER!' to her face. She picked it up and immediately threw it in the bin.

A teenager was dancing by, with headphones in his ears. A blind lady walked by with her stick. A tourist with many suitcases and a map in her hands was rushing by. And finally, an elderly man in a wheelchair was riding by.

Another pin was found laying on the floor on the following day but to another person: Lila Swire. There was a pin on the floor, but this time Lila saw it, ignored it and carried on her morning winter stroll.

A young teenager was dancing with the same headphones which boomed loud music and tripped over the pin; his headphones smashed to pieces. The same blind lady walked by and stepped on the pin causing her to fall down and hurt herself. A tourist walked by and the pin punctured a hole in her suitcase making it flat. Finally, an old man in a wheelchair came, and after the wheel tripping over, his wheelchair went so fast down the pavement, his carer was chasing him.

On the first day no harm was caused because Agnes picked the pin up, however on the second day so much harm was done just because Lila didn't pick a single pin up. In conclusion, a small act of kindness can change a person's life.

***

Zakiyya Suleman
Age 11
Leicestershire, UK

79. Ruby

The Kind Paintbrush

One bright sunny day, a little girl called Willow found a paintbrush at the bottom of her garden. Excitedly, she grabbed her canvas and her special box of paints. She added splashes of colour to her picture. As it began to dry, in a blink, words began to appear. Slowly, the words began to make sentences and that's when Willow knew the paintbrush was magic!

She kept it secret from her family as she didn't want them to take it away from her. It was her special secret… Shhhhhh!

Suddenly, Willow had an amazing idea; she wanted to send people from around the world kind, positive and happy notes. With the help of her magic paintbrush, Willow began writing to anyone who felt sad, worried, upset or angry. When she saw someone upset she told the paintbrush and the paintbrush magically wrote on a special piece of paper,

"You are special, You are unique and
You are brave"

and left it in the pockets of their coats. She watched with amazement as people from around the world started to wear smiles on their faces. They turned their sadness into happiness, their frowns upside down and their worry into enjoyment. They loved their random notes of kindness when they were least expecting them.

Everyone felt the excitement that the world had experienced from these thoughtful and kind notes. Therefore, they continued to write them for other people, to help make them feel special just like the magic paintbrush did.

***

Ruby Isobel Wood
Age 9
Nottinghamshire, UK

"Willow had an amazing idea, she wanted to send people from around the world kind, positive and happy notes. With the help of her magic paintbrush, Willow began writing to anyone who felt sad, worried, upset or angry." – Ruby Wood, Age 9

80. Iris

My Fairy Kindness Story

Once upon a time, there were three fairies; the girl fairies were sisters called Flower and Rosie, the boy fairy was their brother and his name was Leaf.

One day the fairies were out in the magic forest hunting for unicorn magic and they came across a sick unicorn called Sparkle. Sparkle had lost her horn magic because an ugly goat took it away from her and she was very sad because she couldn't get back to her mummy. Unicorns can only fly when they have their power.

The fairies were nice and very kind, they always helped every single animal they could. They were thoughtful because their mummy had taught them to show kindness. They wanted Sparkle to get better and not be sick anymore.

Sparkle's horn power came from her flower necklace which had broken and fallen onto the forest floor. The fairies had a special book that told them how to get the power back into the necklace and fix it.

It all happened very quickly and when the necklace was back around the unicorn's neck, Sparkles horn lit up in rainbow colours and she flew back to her mummy. When she got to her mummy and daddy, they gave her a big cuddle.

Sparkle the unicorn was excited and jumped all around, she wrote in the sky with her rainbow horn and said, "Thank you for being kind". When the fairies saw it, they drew a message back, a little smiley face.

They all lived happily ever after.

***

Iris
Age 4
Nottinghamshire, UK

81. Indie

Kindness is…
Kisses
Kindness is…
Important
Kindness is…
Needed
Kindness is…
Dreams
Kindness is…
Nice
Kindness is…
Everyone
Kindness is…
Sparkles
Kindness is…
Sharing

***

Indie Umney
Age 5
Bedfordshire, UK

82. Andrew

Helping with Kindness

One day, me and Aaron were watching TV with Mummy. An advert came on about poorly children, which upset us. I asked if we could help the children on TV and Aaron shouted, "Me too! I want to help them." Our mummy signed us up to do the Mr Men & Little Miss marathon challenge. Me, Aaron and our little baby sister, Amelia, all started doing challenges with help from Mummy, Daddy, Nanna, Uncle Connor and Aunty Dee. We painted canvases, made cards, did littler picks, did a pick-a-lolly game and lots more!

People kept saying how kind and lovely we were for helping the poorly children. We raised over £540 for The Children with Cancer Charity which made us really happy.

After Christmas, Mummy asked if we could sort through all our old toys so we could give some to other children. Me and Aaron didn't want to, but Mummy told us that at Christmas some children and families didn't even have food, heating or presents. We were shocked! So, we said yes to giving some of our old toys and clothes, and Aaron said, "We need to buy them heaters and they can have money from my wallet to buy food too."

Mummy said if we wanted to raise money again this year, we could buy food and new toys for families for this Christmas. So, we shouted, "YES PLEASE!"

To me, Kindness is helping other people, looking after them, being nice and SMILING!!

***

AJ - Andrew John George Mayers
Age 6
Cheshire, UK

83. Erin

I think kindness is: Caring. Explaining. Setting an example. Playing with someone when they are sad. Helping at home. Showing someone the way if they are lost. Teaching somebody to swim. Helping an old person to cross the road. Giving a friend a hug. Helping people with their shopping. Babysitting. Feeding the wildlife. Holding the door. Giving a compliment. Being kind to your friend. Giving clothes and toys to charity. Giving a homemade gift. Nursing the sick. Smiling to people. Saying please and thank you. Sending a card to cheer someone up. Being polite to your teacher. Apologising when you are wrong. Laughing together. Welcoming a neighbour or pupils in school. Giving without expecting anything back.

Kindness is free!! Spend it always!

***

Erin David
Age 9
Rhondda Cynon Taff, UK

84. Charlie

Kindness Is Contagious

Billy was one of the nicest people you could ever meet. He didn't have a particularly good childhood though, people used to pick on him in secondary and primary school. But he was so kind to people, and he didn't want them to feel the way he did.

One morning, Billy woke up and looked at his watch to see the time. It was 9:27, a good time to wake up. He put on his old slippers and dressing gown and went downstairs for breakfast.

Billy got dressed after breakfast and headed out for some shopping. On his walk down to the shop, he noticed a homeless woman. Billy walked up to her and gave her five pounds. "Here you go," said Billy. "Oh, my goodness, thank you so much. God bless you!" the homeless woman said to Billy.

When Billy was paying for his shopping, he noticed a woman who was trying to buy a birthday present for her son, but then found out she could not afford it. The lady got really upset, and a bit teary. "Hold on a sec lad," Billy said to the guy at the till. Billy walked over to the lady, "It's okay," he said to her, and gave her twenty-five pounds to pay for the gift. The woman was shocked.

Billy smiled and turned around back to his till. Everybody should help others; it will make yours and their life better…

***

Charlie Room
Age 10
Kent, UK

85. Holly

Being kind means that you help someone if they are feeling bad about something. When I'm kind to someone it makes them feel happy and it makes me feel happy too. If someone falls over it's best to go and help them because that's being kind. If someone doesn't have anyone to play with, go and ask them if they want to play with you. If someone doesn't have as many things as you, share them, even if you might not want to, because that's being kind. If someone doesn't have any food you should share your food. Don't call people names or be mean just because someone is a bit different to you. Even if people are different to you it's best to try and make friends with them and you might find something you like about them. Everybody's different and that's ok; everyone has different things that are good about them or that they are good at. You should always be kind and show people how much you care for them.

***

Holly Finnegan
Age 7
Nottinghamshire, UK

86. Sinai

Kindness to me is when:

K- keeping my toys tidy so no one gets hurt

I- in the summer, helping Mummy buy yummy ice-cream

N- not fighting with my little sister

D- doing what Mummy asks me to do

N- neatly putting the DVDs in a nice pile when Mummy asks me to

E- eating all the food that Mummy gives me

S- sharing with Zia

S- sleeping on time.

***

Sinai Isabella
Age 5
West Midlands, UK

87. Ruby

Once upon a time, there was a little girl called Ruby Rainbow. Her mum said she needed to go to school that day and we had to hurry hurry to get there.

Ruby said, "Today I am going to be Kind and Friendly".

She ran and ran till she got to school.

She loved school and that day was playing with some princesses, till a little girl came and asked her, "Can I play with your princesses?" and she said, "Yes".

The little girl was really happy, and that made Ruby Rainbow really kind.

***

Ruby Jedras
Age 5
London, UK

88. Esme

Kindness

Kindness isn't something that we buy. Kindness is something we give. There are different ways we can be kind.

Being kind to others isn't just buying a gift, we can be kind by giving someone a listening ear or a friendly chat, by being there to help in a difficult situation, or just by giving a stranger a smile we can make their day brighter. Sometimes my mum buys flowers in town and then asks me to choose someone to give them to, this is called a random act of kindness that leaves the chosen one feeling special.

Being kind to our world is very important. We can do this by using less plastic, stopping deforestation and using less fossil fuels which pollute our atmosphere. All of these things merge together to create global warming which is something we need to stop! I help our environment by litter picking at school, I collect playground litter and put it in the bin.

Being kind to animals is important to me. Many species are becoming extinct because of the way humans are treating them and their natural habitats. Once again, global warming plays a part in this. This year I am holding a cake sale to raise money for Shark Conservation.

Ultimately, we need to be kind to ourselves. By believing in ourselves, being positive in all we do, allowing ourselves to rest when we need to and expressing our feelings, we can continue to be kind to our world.

***

Esme Bradley
Age 10
Devon, UK

89. Daisy

KINDNESS RULES!

Kindness is a something. A something very special.
A person. A helpful person. A caring person.
An emotion. A loving emotion. A joyful emotion.
Keeping calm when all around is in commotion.

Moving a tired bee onto a pretty flower,
Some water for a drooping plant.
A simple smile,
A loving hug as big as a mile.

A kiss and a plaster on a hurt knee.
Spending time with someone who is alone.
Listening with a caring ear,
Wiping away a soulful tear.

Giving a compliment for no reason.
A thank you card for a present given.
A hankie for a snotty nose.
Forgiving someone with repose.

Saying thank you for your food.
Raising money for a worthy cause.
Sharing a joke with someone who is sad.
Saying I love you to a tired Mum or Dad.

No matter how young or old,
No matter how big or small,
Kindness comes in all shapes and sizes,
As your kindness comes out, their happiness rises.

***

Daisy Grace Leftwich
Age 11
Devon, UK

90. Gracie

It all began under the diamond clear ocean.

The sun shone through the water, as the tide gently flowed over the golden sand. There lived a mermaid, she had a wonderful sky-blue tail and beautiful golden hair as soft as silk. The mermaids name was Coral. Coral lived in a rainbow castle - made of coral - and that's where she got her name.

Coral loved animals, she had three pets, a goldfish called Goldie, a seahorse called Bouncer and a starfish called Bongo. But Coral loved ALL animals more than anything, in fact, she enjoyed caring for everything in the ocean.

One day Coral heard a creature shouting, "Help, help! My fin is broken! What can I do?!"
She immediately swam to see who needed help. Coral swam as fast as she could and found the deafening shouts of a SHARK!

She saw the shark had a broken fin! So, she shouted for all her pets to bring some plasters. Coral was really kind, although the shark was the meanest shark in the ocean. She plastered his fin so it could repair itself, the shark was very ungrateful and swam off without a thank you.

One day, Coral was playing in the ocean, when all of a sudden, a net dropped down on top of her! There was a boat pulling the net up and she started to shout for help. The shark recognised the mermaids voice and swam as fast as he could to her. The shark bit a hole in the net, so Coral could swim free.

Coral never thought she would become best friends with that mean old shark... Kindness is never wasted.

***

Gracie Rose Wardega
Age 7
Nottinghamshire, UK

"She saw the shark had a broken fin! So, she shouted for all her pets to bring some plasters. Coral was really kind, although the shark was the meanest shark in the ocean. She plastered his fin so it could repair itself."– Gracie Rose Wardega, Age 7

91. Stefan

When someone is kind to me it makes me happy, excited, and I like them even more.

I feel excellent when I'm kind to somebody else. Playing with my friend Iona at school and being her best friend is kind and makes me happy.

I share my toys with Gracie and Beatrix; being kind makes us all happy.

***

Stefan Alexander Wardega
Age 5
Nottinghamshire, UK

92. Maria

Secondo me a volte si confonde la gentilezza con l'educazione, con il dire "per favore" o "grazie", restituire gli oggetti prestati non significa "essere gentili", ma essere educati.

Si è gentili donando un sorriso che può cambiare la giornata di qualcuno o dando un abbraccio di conforto. Secondo me la gentilezza è simile all'educazione, ma non è un suo sinonimo. Essere gentili non ci costa nulla, eppure molte persone proprio non ci riescono. Se tutti fossimo gentili, più della metà dei problemi che affliggono l'uomo non si sarebbero.

Un gesto di vera gentilezza, d'altronde, ne richiama sempre un altro.

Maria Elena Nardini
Scuola Secondaria di Primo Grado
Istituto V. Alfieri. Spinetta Marengo

***

In my opinion, kindness is sometimes confused with good manners, like saying "please" or "thank you"; for example, returning borrowed items does not mean 'being kind', but is being polite.

Kindness is giving a smile that can change someone's day or by giving a comforting hug. In my opinion, kindness is similar to good manners, but it is not the same. Being nice doesn't cost us anything, yet many people are not. If we were all kind, more than half of the problems facing man would not have happened.

A gesture of true kindness always calls for another.

Maria Elena Nardini
First Grade Secondary School
V. Alfieri Institute. Spinetta Marengo

***

Maria Elena Nardini
Age 11
Alessandria, Italy

93. Sara

La parola "gentilezza" in questi ultimi anni non è molto conosciuta. Essere gentili per me significa avere cura delle persone e dei loro sentimenti, non solo a parole non ma con piccoli gesti o anche solo chiedendogli come stiano, tirando loro su il morale. Sapere come sta davvero una persona chiedendogli se voglia parlare, di qualsiasi cosa, questa è la gentilezza, come il saluto o il "per favore" sono l'educazione.

Ultimamente mi sono accorta di come le persone non usino la gentilezza quando di devono confrontare tra loro, nasce subito l'aggressione e si usano toni sgarbati. Si potrebbe pensare che la gentilezza sia un dono, che alcuni lo possiedono dalla nascita e che a certe persone non sia donato.

La gentilezza invece, è un modo di vivere, è l'educazione che ci hanno insegnato i nostri genitori. Oggi si conosce la prepotenza, quella si che viene usata spesso! Quando noi siamo gentili e magari con un sorriso sulle labbra, ogni cosa chiesta, ogni gesto, diventano positivi, le persone attorno a noi sono influenzate da questo atteggiamento. Dicono che la gentilezza è contagiosa con una bella risata.

Forse a scuola, tra le varie materie che studiamo, bisognerebbe inserire un corso di 'gentilezza' per tutti, sarei curiosa di sapere quanti di noi otterrebbero la sufficienza!

La gentilezza si può manifestare interessandoci alle persone che si stanno vicine, diamo sempre tutto per scontato, pensiamo che se una persona sorride e svolge le sue mansioni quotidiane sia sereno. Molte volte basterebbe chiedere "come stai?", "come ti senti?", "tutto bene?". Questa è gentilezza, per non diventare persone egoiste.

Quante volte un piccolo gesto di gentilezza e di amore può cambiare la giornata oppure farci sentire importanti e amati.

La gentilezza non costa nulla.

Sara Piscopello
Scuola Secondaria di Primo Grado
Istituto V. Alfieri. Spinetta Marengo

***

The word "kindness" in recent years is not widely known. Being kind to me means taking care of people and their feelings, not only with words but with small gestures or even just asking them how they are, raising their spirits. Knowing how a person really is, asking if he wants to talk about anything, this is kindness, in the same way as saying "please" is good manners.

Lately, I have noticed how people do not use kindness when they have to confront one another, they become immediately aggressive using rude tones. One might think that kindness is a gift, that some have it since birth, yet some people still do not possess it.

Kindness is a way of life; it is the education that our parents taught us. Instead today we experience more arrogance and it is more often used! When we are kind and perhaps with a smile on our lips, everything asked for, every gesture, becomes positive, the people around us are influenced by this attitude. They say that kindness is contagious like laughter.

Maybe at school, among the various subjects we study, we should include a course of 'kindness' for everyone, I would be curious to know how many of us would pass!

Kindness can be manifested by being interested in people who are close to us, we always take everything for granted, we think that if a person smiles and performs his daily tasks, he is serene. Many times, it would be enough to ask, "How are you?", "How are you feeling?", "Are you ok?". Not to be selfish is true kindness.

How many times a small gesture of kindness and love can change the day or make us feel important and loved.

Kindness costs nothing.

Sara Piscopello
Scuola Secondaria di Primo Grado
Istituto V. Alfieri. Spinetta Marengo

***

Sara Piscopello
Age 11
Alessandria, Italy

94. Daisy

Once upon a time there was a fairy; a kindness fairy. The kindness fairy was called Blossom. She wore a blossom dress and blossom flowers in her hair. Whenever she walked past people, she made them kind.

One day, Blossom met a giant and that giant was not very happy and not very kind either. He used to snatch other people's food and drink all their drink. He didn't have any food or drink of his own because he was unkind, so people wouldn't share.

Blossom tried to make the giant share with others. She waved her magic wand and said the secret words. The secret words were, "Be kind, be kind, Giant be kind".

The magic spell didn't work.

Blossom thought, 'I will be kind to the giant'. She shared her food and drink and made the giant a lovely picnic.

The giant felt happy and kind. He promised to never take anyone's food or drink away again. The kindness fairy and the giant became best friends. They lived happily ever after. The end.

***

Daisy Whittaker
Age 6
Devon, UK

"Blossom thought, 'I will be kind to the giant'. She shared her food and drink and made the giant a lovely picnic. The kindness fairy and the giant became best friends." – Daisy Whittaker, Age 6

95. Noah

Be kind to everyone

Be kind to Mummy,
Be kind to octopuses,
Be kind to kangaroos,
Be kind to bears,

Be kind to Nanny & Grandpa,
Be kind to dogs,
Be kind to rhinos,
Be kind to tables,

Be kind to cats,
Be kind to elephants,
Be kind to chairs,
Be kind to bumblebees,

Be kind to flowers,
Be kind to tigers,
Be kind to dinosaurs,
Be kind to trees,

Be kind to you,
Be kind to me!

***

Noah Whittaker
Age 4
Devon, UK

96. Erin

"Kindness is the best
And it all comes from the chest.
If you don't show it
A kind, loving heart will split.
All you bullies out there, be kind
So, use your clever mind.
Don't be unkind YOU
Don't make someone go boohoo.
Kindness is like first love
It can change a life.
With a miracle and a promise
To wipe away sorrows and strife.
Use your amazing brain
Otherwise people will have pain.
The ones who are kind starts with you and me
So, don't knock down someone's tree.
Come on, you have a heart,
If you don't use it another will part.
So, stand out
And without a doubt.
You'll find a friend
And I'm sure your friendship will never end."

***

Erin Kasas
Age 8
Nottinghamshire, UK

97. Hayyan

Kindness Starts at Home

Kindness, kindness is everywhere.

Kindness is in our hearts; kindness is in our homes.

My Dad helps my Mama at home. My Mama is a freelancer. She is working from home. My Dad takes care of me and my 18-month-old sister.

I am making a kindness calendar of random acts with the help of my Mom and Dad, for all of us. We will perform according to it. This will be fun and goodness as well.

My late Baba (my Dad's younger brother) was very kind to everyone. I lost my Baba on 12th December 2019 due to a bike accident. My whole family is very sad. I am also sad. He brought me my favourite things. I am always missing all the flavoured biscuits he gave me as a surprise. Every year, all of us celebrated my birthday happily on 8th January. We did not celebrate my birthday this year like my previous birthdays. My Baba blew up balloons for me on every birthday. There were no balloons this year. I always remember him and his kindness.

I have learnt how to be kind from my family. I dedicate

becoming a child author of this "Kindness" book to my Baba. He was very happy when I became a published child author in the "Happiness" book.

***

In loving memory of 'Baba'.
Kamran Hussain.

***

Hayyan Rizwan
Age 6
Gilgit Baltistan, Pakistan

98. Maeve

Veel mensen denken dat vriendelijkheid of aardig zijn betekent dat je dat moet zijn voor andere mensen en dieren, hun gelukkig moet maken en het 'aardig zijn ding' doen.

Maar ik denk dat het allerbelangrijkste is - (dat is wat mijn moeder me ook verteld heeft) - om aardig voor mezelf te zijn. Ik moet vooral mezelf leuk vinden - mezelf behandelen zoals ik iemand anders zou behandelen.

Ik hou veel van mijn oma's en opa, familie en mijn huisdieren en mijn vrienden, ik ben ook echt aardig voor ze.

Vorige week zei een mevrouw in de supermarkt: "Je hebt zo'n knap koppie." Ik vind dat echt lief. Ik ken haar niet eens. En... Hou gewoon je mond als je niet iets aardigs kunt zeggen. Je moet gewoon aardig tegen anderen praten. Gemeen zijn is niet oké. En een andere mevrouw in de Lidl gaf me stickers, zodat ik nog meer knuffels kon verzamelen.

Toen onze kitten ffiona vorige week haar heup brak, doneerden sommige mensen wat geld voor haar operatie. Dat was echt super aardig.

Om de natuur aardig te behandelen moet je plastic en andere rommel opruimen. Dan gaan de dieren niet dood. Het is echt niet zo moeilijk om te doen hoor!

Je vriendinnen jouw snoep geven is ook echt aardig.

Met iemand die nieuw is op school gaan praten en vragen of ze mijn vriendje willen zijn.

Ik zeg altijd 'Hoi' tegen mensen op straat.

Ik ruim mijn oude speelgoed op en geef het dan aan andere kinderen.

Ik vind echt dat ik aardig ben.

***

People think kindness means being nice to other people and animals, making them happy, and doing the kindness thing.

But I think the most important is - that's what my mum tells me - to be kind to myself. I have to like myself - treating myself as I would anyone else. I love my grannies and grandpa, family and my pets and my friends, I am kind to them too.

Last week a lady at the supermarket said: "You have such a pretty face." I think that's kind of her. I don't even know her. If you can't be kind, please shut up. You have to talk kind to others. Mean is not okay. And another lady in the Lidl gave me stickers, so I could collect more toys.

When our kitten Ffiona broke her hip last week, some people gave us money for her surgery. That was super kind.

To be kind to nature you have to pick up litter, so animals don't die. It's not that hard to do.

Giving your friend your candy is kind.

I talk to someone new at school and ask if they want to be my friend.

I always say 'Hi' to people in the street.

I clean up my old toys and give them to other kids.

I think I am kind.

***

Maeve Marin van der Velden
Age 6
Rotterdam, The Netherlands

99. Heidi

Kindness is a big act and could have a massive impact on someone's day (and maybe yours).

I think kindness is a great thing. It is a quality of being generous to others around you. Sometimes people forget what kindness is, which doesn't usually end up in a good situation. Which is why we have World Kindness Day on the 13th of November.

Spreading kindness doesn't mean buying someone something expensive, all it is, is a little compliment that you say to someone when they're sad or happy or just whenever!

Kindness comes with a lot of different characteristics like being aware of the needs of others and being there to support them.

The world would be a terribly sad place to live in if there was no such thing as kindness. If there was no kindness, there would be no such thing as friendships and relationships.

Kindness is treating someone with respect and making sure they feel welcome and wanted. Treating someone how you would want to be treated.

Sometimes kids are mean to others because they don't know what kindness is, themselves. When your friendship group are picking on an individual, you must take charge of the situation and point out that what they're doing isn't necessarily kind.

Try and set a daily goal to make several people smile in one day, because you never know what is happening at home.

Try to change people's mindsets to be kinder to others around you.

Love is kindness.

***

Heidi Williams
Age 11
Greater Manchester, UK

100. Phoebe

What Kindness Means to Me

To me, kindness means helping someone, no matter what.

Kindness and being nice are very different. Being nice is when you smile or compliment someone, sometimes expecting something back. Being kind is a lot nicer. (But being nice is still good).

Being kind is when you listen to someone or buy a nice little gift for someone. Kindness helps everyone, even if they don't want it sometimes.

People won't expect your kindness but that doesn't mean they don't need it.

When I was going through a sad time with my dad passing away, I refused to have kindness, but I really did need it and when I did allow people to talk with me about my feelings I felt a lot better.

So, I think kindness is the best thing you can do for someone but never force your kindness on someone.

***

Phoebe McLinden
Age 11
Cheshire, UK

101. Aiza

Being kind is natural. It comes from within. It can be learned by practice and from our parents.

For showing kindness, all you want is a good and a big heart. We must be kind to all living beings. We must treat everyone equally.

For doing kindness, some people give secret donations to any person or organization. It gives them inner peace and satisfaction. We should also behave well with each other.

Children must learn this value from a very early stage. They must know how to behave with humans as well as animals. They must provide food and shelter to animals as they are also living beings.

"When you are kind to
someone in trouble,
you hope they will
remember and be kind
to someone else, and
it will become like a
wildfire."
– *Whoopi Goldberg.*

It is a very necessary element to understand while living in a society because kindness also helps us to bring the feelings of brotherhood amongst us.

We must also be kind to old persons and help them in doing their chores because they are weak and old.

Every religion on Earth talks about kindness, we must try to adopt good manners and behaviors to promote kindness and peace in the society and world we are living in.

***

Aiza Mazhar
Age 6
Karachi, Pakistan

102. Sawyere

When I see someone alone I play with them, that is kindness. I think kindness is when I give my mommy flowers. I make my sister feel better when I think she feels sad, that is being kind. Kindness is helping my family around the house and in the yard. I would tell anyone that wanted to be kind, to have nice manners and surprise people with a present; Maybe a Frozen 2 Elsa dress! I smile at everybody because it makes me feel good and it is kind.

Being kind is playing fun games with my friends at school or outside. My mommy is kind to me too. She always makes me feel better and makes me smile. I love to be around people that are kind. Kindness makes me feel good, great, smiley and happy. It makes me want to be kind all of the time. I love kindness.

***

Sawyere Gibson
Age 4
Florida, USA

103. Elsie

Some times when people have been kind to me:

- Once in a lesson, a friend of mine trapped my finger in between a chair and a table, then felt very sorry and gave me two jelly bears, so I forgave her.

- Once, my brother came home with two mint chewing gums, one for me and one for him. But then, he gave them both to me, so I felt really happy, so I gave him the two jelly bears that my friend gave to me when she trapped my finger. It was a good job that I didn't eat my jelly bears!

Some times when I have been kind to other people:

- I gave my mini petit gateau to my brother because he insisted that he wanted his one to be cooked for one minute more than it was supposed to, so his became hard and tough. He got sad so I gave him my lovely and runny one and he was very pleased to get my one.

- I was in my brother's bedroom and I knocked his favourite Top Gear money box and because it was ceramic, it broke into small pieces. I came downstairs and told him what had happened, and he started crying, so I did as well.

Then my mum said, "Well done for telling the truth, you could have said it was Archie". So, my dad then glued it back together, but there were still pieces missing.

***

Elsie Brown
Age 11
Mortágua, Portugal

104. Carolyne

The word kindness means many things and has many meanings depending on people's experiences. For example, for me, kindness reminds me of people such as my mama. It is not only the things that she does for me and others but also the kind words she always has and more. Kindness can also be an action. Patience and kindness can go a very long way, it can turn someone's day around. There are many examples of kindness actions such as complementing a random stranger or taking someone's cart back to the return at the grocery store.

There can also be multiple reasons why you believe that you are kind. Since I think that the definition of kind actions can be varied depending on the person, that means there are many choices for you to do a kind action. For example, I believe that I am kind because of the kind actions I have performed which include actions such as volunteering in my community and always complimenting others.

Kindness is ultimately a feeling. Kindness makes me feel gratitude and happiness for people and situations. What this means is it could be anything. For me, a mixture of gratitude and happiness is what I feel when I am with my friends at a rehearsal. I look forward to seeing my team because they are kind as well. Being kind brings more kindness into my life. It is pretty easy when I am around my nieces, Sawyere and Suttyn; they are always happy and doing nice things and hanging out with them can turn my day around.

In conclusion, kindness can stretch to a wide array of feelings and things, so you have many options to be kind. What is your definition of kindness?

***

Carolyne Miner
Age 14
Florida, USA

105. Isabella

Aardig… Betekend voor mij aardig zijn tegen mensen, dieren en de hele wereld.

Als je zelf aardig bent dan zijn mensen en dieren ook aardig tegen jou.

Mijn vriendinnen op school zijn geweldig en ook heel aardig. Ze zijn lief en helpen en troosten mij.
Dat is aardig zijn…

Laatst op school pakte een kindje iets van mij af… dat was niet aardig. Maar een jongetje zag dat en die pakte zonder iets te zeggen het voor mij terug! Dat was wel écht super aardig.

Binnenkort krijg ik een puppy waar ik super goed voor ga zorgen. Dan zal zij mij beschermen en veel met mij knuffelen omdat Lilly dan onvoorwaardelijk van mij houdt.

Ik weet zeker dat mijn puppy echt heel erg aardig voor mij zal zijn!

***

Kindness means - you need to be kind to people, animals and the entire world.

If you are kind yourself then people and animals are kind to you, too.

My friends at school are also very amazing and kind. They are sweet and help and comfort me. That's what kindness means to me…

The other day at school someone took something from me… That was not nice at all. But a boy saw it and got it back for me - without saying a word! That was kind.

I will get a puppy soon. I will take super good care of her. Then she will protect me and hug me lots, because she will love me unconditionally.

I am sure my puppy Lilly has kindness written all over her!

***

Isabella Kuiper
Age 6
Rotterdam, The Netherlands

106. Harriet

BE KIND

When someone is sad
Be kind

When someone is hurting
Be kind

If someone has fallen
Be kind

If someone is poorly
Be kind

If someone is frightened
Be kind

If someone is lonely
Be kind

If someone is struggling
Be kind

If someone is different
Be kind

If someone is hungry
Be kind

If someone is mean
Be kind

If someone hurts you
Be kind

If you can be anything
Be kind

Be kind to everybody.

***

Harriet Taylor
Age 7
Derbyshire, UK

107. Violet

Kindness

Kissing your family
Illuminating, be a light when people are in the dark
Neighbours, greet your neighbour and everyone you meet
Dreams, help people achieve their dreams
Nurture, look after someone and yourself
Endless love for family and friends
Smile at somebody as it's contagious, if you do, everyone will.
Superpower, Kindness will be your superpower!

What is Kindness?

Kindness is love
Kindness is nurture
Kindness is help
Kindness is strong
Kindness is standing up for friends
Kindness is lovely to have
Kindness is nice
Kindness is caring
Kindness is you

Kindness is not unloved
Kindness is not bullying
Kindness is not bad
Kindness is not weak
Kindness is not mean
Kindness is not leaving someone behind
Kindness is not terrible
Kindness is not hurting people
Kindness is you

***

Violet Taylor
Age 10
Derbyshire, UK

108. Oscar

'The Thing'

To The Scientist,
Sometimes I get 'The Thing' and I wanted to tell you about my discoveries so that you can help other people if they get 'The Thing' too. 'The Thing' is when I feel extremely cross and sad, all at the same time. When you get 'The Thing', you might say bad words and cry!

Here's some advice for other children if they get 'The Thing':

- Get into a safe quiet space (like a cupboard!)
- Be with someone and don't be alone
- Have hugs and kisses
- Get your teddy
- When you are feeling calmer, have a bath – I like using a bath bomb too!
- Have some nice smells in a diffuser
- Maybe sleep in your mum and dad's bed

We hope this is helpful. Have a nice day!

***

Oscar Goffer (with help from Mum, Louise)
Age 6
Leicestershire, UK

109. Maisie

Maisie's Kindness

Once there was a girl called Maisie (me). I was a kind and loving person to family and friends. I always thought about other people before myself and never gave up. No matter what my mother or father said, I always listened.

One day at school, I thought about my friend, Michalina, and how she had never had a birthday party before. So, I decided to give her one.

A SURPRISE PARTY!!!

I sent a letter out to Michalina's best friend Ella. Ella was so excited she could barely keep it a secret. All that Michalina knew was that she was coming to my house for a play. In preparation, I made a pink cake with three layers.

When Michalina arrived, she was amazed with how much effort I had put into it. We made friendship bracelets, had a disco party, played party games, opened presents and ate the party food. When the cake was brought out, she was very thankful of my work of art.

Sadly, the party then ended. Everyone went home sad to say goodbye.

After the surprise party, me and my brother, Oscar, still had a lot of energy. So, we partied on into the night till we had to go to bed.

On Monday, when we went back to school, Michalina had a surprise in return. She had bought me and Ella a present each.

This is a true story of kindness.

***

Maisie Goffer
Age 9
Leicestershire, UK

110. Anaiah

The Story of The Sad Unicorn and The Kind Little Girl

One night a child called Anaiah was scared and lonely, she cuddled Sparkle. Anaiah's pet Unicorn, Sparkle, wanted to fly but she couldn't because she was frightened.

Anaiah had a kind heart; she wanted to help her and had a great idea. She made sparkle dust for her pet Unicorn. Anaiah used sequins, glitter, flour, sparkles, sugar and sprinkles to make the recipe. One was too dull, one was too sparkly, and one was just right.

Anaiah thought she was feeling sad, so she gave her a cuddle. Sparkle ate the potion and flied into space.

***

Anaiah
Age 6

III. Lily-Jane

Kindness is something you can find in everyone. Even though they don't act like it around you or don't look like they do, they still have kindness in them.
It is not just humans that are kind, animals can also be kind in their own way.
You can be kind to anyone, not just loved ones or people you know.

To me, kindness is helping others, sharing, looking out for others and making people feel better when they're sad.

***

Lily-Jane Townley
Age 9
Lancashire, UK

112. Kayla

Kindness means...

- Help people when needed
- Helping others
- Always help a person when they are hurt
- Ask people if they are ok when they look hurt or seem alone
- Being nice to other people
- Being friendly
- Being helpful

Ways to be kind...

- Smile
- Hold a door open for someone else
- Give someone a hug
- Pick up litter
- Plant a tree
- Give away my old toys
- Share with others

When I think of kindness I think of:

K- Kind-hearted
I- Incredible
N- Nice
D- Different
N- Nurture
E- Environment
S- Smile
S- Special

***

Kayla Moore
Age 7
Victoria, Australia

113. Marko

Kindness. For me and probably for many other people who have hearts, kindness means a lot. Kindness is seen in many things. It's always nice to have a kind friend by your side; somebody who understands you completely; somebody you can always tell everything, no matter if it's good or bad. Being kind isn't easy because if you dress well or if you have much money, it doesn't mean you are kind. Kindness is when you share that money with others who don't have it. I want to say that kindness comes from within, from the heart. And not everyone can have that heart. You are born with it and you live with it every day of your life. Kindness is maybe the most important human quality. Through kindness we become better versions of ourselves.

***

Marko Cvijanovic
Age 14
The Republic of Srpska, Bosnia & Herzegovina

114. Minnie

Kindness is for helping people if they are hurt. If they fall over you can help them and show them where the star is. The star will make them better.

Then you can get an ice pack and wash it away if it's bleeding. Then, you get a plaster, so they feel better.

When someone is kind to me, it makes me happy because I like smiling at people. When I smile, people love my smile. I like people's smiles; they make me feel good.

When I'm kind to Daddy, I help him if he falls off his motorbike; I will get him a plaster. Listening is kind too, and teaching is kind because we have to listen and learn. My teacher helps me. Listening helps us work and concentrate, and feel we're heard and concentrate our brain.

Sharing and caring.

Sharing is caring. We share to be kind because it's nice. We have to do that because others might not want to play with us. We also share when someone doesn't have as much as us. Everyone likes sharing.

Kindness is when you ask me, "Minnie are you OK?" My heart is kind. Ted Ted says kindness is for loving. We love people when they do smiles at our face. My Ted Ted is kind to me, she sleeps with me to make me feel safe. I love Ted Ted and Ted Ted loves me. I love myself.

This week I was helpful and that was kind. You have to be helpful for who you are and for what you got.

***

Minnie Taylor
Age 5
UK

115. Tess

All About Kindness

Kindness means the different helpful ways to live in the world.

Kindness is being respectful to our world and animals by not throwing rubbish on the floor or in the sea. Being kind to animals is not killing them and being gentle with them.

There are also some things that you can do to help people, helping them up if they have fallen over and showing good manners like saying, "Please", "Thank you" and "No, thank you".

To be kind and show that you are a good friend you can congratulate them if they win and help them if they are struggling.

To help teachers you can tidy up the classroom, sit down on the carpet and listen carefully to what they say and follow the rules.

I think the kindest thing in the world is to show good manners and to be gentle with the planet and everything in it.

***

Tess Lupton
Age 7
Lancashire, UK

"I think the kindest thing in the world is to show good manners and to be gentle with the planet and everything in it." – Tess Lupton, Age 7

116. Sofia

Kindness makes me smiley and happy, like when the sun shines.

I like making other people happy by being friendly, by smiling at them and holding the door open for them.

I care about my friends and I am kind to them because I let them join in and we take turns when playing our games.

Sharing is being kind and I like to share my toys and games with my friends.

I am kind to my pets by being gentle and caring with them and I give them lots of love so that they are happy.

I am kind and thoughtful with my family and friends and I think about how my actions will make other people feel. Kindness means treating other people how you would want them to treat you.

It makes me feel good to be kind!

***

Sofia Steadman
Age 8
Lancashire, UK

117. Jake

KINDNESS

The Dictionary definition of Kindness is – 'The Quality of being friendly, generous and considerate'.

To me 'Kindness' means…

Friendship and Family
Helping people when I can
Sharing with others
Being nice to animals
Looking after our planet
Smiling at everyone I meet
Looking out for one and other
A random act:- doing something for someone 'just because it will make them smile'.

I pledge to be kind to everyone I meet and look out for others.

***

Jake Swift
Age 8
Doncaster, UK

118. Alfie

10 Easy Ways to Be Kind

1. Offering to help someone if they are struggling or busy
2. Sharing is caring and can make someone really happy
3. Giving compliments to people
4. Inviting people to join in when they are on their own
5. Explain or show people what to do if they need help
6. Encourage people when they are trying new things or unsure
8. Giving presents, cards or letters which make people happy and lets them know you are thinking of them
8. Asking people how they feel
9. Smile at people
10. Treat people how you want to be treated

There are many more ways you can be kind and maybe you can make your own list and tick something off every day.

Imagine how you will feel from being so kind

***

Alfie Kavanagh
Age 6
Lancashire, UK

119. Eva

Kindness is making people happy, you can do anything to be kind like giving a compliment, smiling or just giving them a hug.

When you are kind you feel great. It doesn't cost anything to be kind, you just simply do it!

Being kind to someone makes them kinder to others and all that kindness adds up to making the world a better place.

Imagine yourself in this situation, what would you do, would you follow this example, or do you have your own idea?

You are in class and asked to work as a team to complete a task, you each have a part that you must do.

There is one kid who is being really bossy and won't let another kid do their part, they are telling them they are doing it wrong, it looks messy, they don't know what they are doing and that they could do it better themselves.

Everyone is starting to feel down and aren't enjoying what should be a fun activity because of how this one kid is behaving.

Do you:

A. Keep quiet?
B. Stand up to the kid being mean and tell them the effect they are having on everyone, then compliment the kid who is upset?
C. Something different but try to make the upset kid happy by being kind to them?

So long as you don't do A then that's the right answer!

Be kind every minute of every day and make a difference in the world

***

Eva Kavanagh
Age 7
Lancashire, UK

120. Eden

I think kindness is helping other people. When someone is kind to me, I feel happy. When I am kind to someone, I feel good.

One day, I was playing on the trim trail at school and I tripped, then my friend got the teacher. I said, "Thank you", and I was grateful.

One night, my little sister was in bed and wanted a toy to cuddle. So, I gave her my toy cat, Emerald. I think she felt comforted and she fell asleep.

Kindness is also being able to be selfless. Although I also wanted my cat, Emerald, I gave it to my little sister to cuddle. This was me being selfless and therefore being kind.

What I think is kindness is a gift.

My poem of kindness:

Kindness is a gift,
A gift we should cherish.
Being helpful, being selfless.
Kindness is a gift,
We should take care of it.

***

Eden Phoebe Trendall-Morrison
Age 9
Northamptonshire, UK

121. Avalonne

Kindness

Kindness is where you care or help out for a good cause.

I think being kind is one of the most important values in you and your environment, the golden rule in life is 'treat people in life how you want to be treated'. What it means is be kind to people and they will be kind back.

It's not always easy to be kind, but did you know that being kind to someone will make you feel good about yourself and improve your mood!

I believe it's very important you are kind and respectful to people and it's even more important to be kind when you see someone down and gloomy, even if they are mean to you. You need to keep trying to be friendly, even if it's hard.

Kindness is the best value anyone can have.

If we were all kind to each other, there would be less fighting and arguments, and it would be a more peaceful world. I think this world should be more peaceful and calm, and there shouldn't be any more arguments, and that's why being so kind is so very important.

Treat people how you want to be treated and people will treat you how you want to be treated.

So be kind at work, school, playground, town.

"BE KIND WHEREVER YOU ARE AND KINDNESS WILL COME TO YOU."

Treat people in life how you want to be treated. If we're kind, then we can live a happier life.

***

Avalonne Rose Trendall-Morrison
Age 10
Northamptonshire, UK

122. Alex

Keep going.
I believe in you.
Niceness to people.
DVD time with munchies.
Not letting people be sad.
Everything is going to be great.
Smiles all around.
Special hugs for family and friends.

***

Alex Killeen
Age 15
Warwickshire, UK

123. Finn

Kindness Shoes

Timmy made a shoe choice one morning. Let's see which ones he chose.

Timmy is helping Matt and Eva make a massive hotel for hedgehogs to keep warm. They had their wellies on for this job.

Matt and Eva were watering some plants for the hedgehog hotel and Jimmy threw their plants away. Matt and Eva were sad.

Timmy wanted to cheer them up. He said they could go to the river to watch the boats as they had their wellies on too!

Timmy needed help with directions to the river. He asked Jimmy, who said, "Go away! I know the way but I'm not going to tell you."

Timmy saw a girl with a kind smile. He went over to ask her, and she was really helpful.

They asked Jimmy, "Would you like to come with us? We have wellies for you if you want to?"

Jimmy was pleased to be asked, and said, "I didn't think I could go as I didn't have the right shoes. That's why I was being mean. I am sorry!"

Timmy, Matt, Eva and Jimmy got to the river and everyone was happy.

Who do you think is wearing the kindness shoes?

- Timmy – helped Matt, Eva and Jimmy feel better.
- Matt and Eva – helped the hedgehogs and included Jimmy.
- The girl – smiled kindly and helped them.
- Jimmy – said sorry and realised he had been unkind.

So, this story isn't really about shoes but about the choices we make.

Please be kind.

***

Finn Dinsdale
Age 6
Kent, UK

"Timmy wanted to cheer them up. He said they could go to the river to watch the boats as they had their wellies on too!" – Finn Dinsdale, Age 6

124. Samuel

Kindness

Kindness is not a word, or a phrase that helps. It's not possible for you to see it in your hands or throw it around like a bouncy ball.

Kindness is a quality… A possibility.

You learn this word in your childhood, as a simple word. An everyday word. A lame childish thing that could make a better world. Even if you think that it is a fantastic word, you'll probably forget it in 30 seconds. But really, to use it you need to use the word as an object, and the object as a tool. And use it ALWAYS.

To use 'Kindness' in everyday life is to use it frequently. Create an everyday 'ahhh' moment is what we're told.

Use it daily, use it wisely and at a good time: if someone's in the middle of something, don't interrupt them from their task / fun. Instead wait for the right moment to give your 'kindness'. Waiting for the *right time* also can bring a greater impact.

Use your tool on people, and you may become friends with many people on your journey. They become your steppingstones. Some you may wish to leave behind, whilst others you'd like to take with you on your journey of life. Some stones may pop up and some may slowly drift away beneath your feet. But throughout your journey, always remember that you have your 'kindness tool'.

***

Samuel Waxman
Age 9
Buckinghamshire, UK

125. Helena

Kindness ABC's

Ask someone to play
Bring a magic wand to make your worries go away
Cuddle someone until they smile
Dance with someone to make them giggle
Encourage someone to join in
Find something nice to say
Give a smile to brighten their day
Helping them when they need it
I give them my toys to play with
Jig with them to a song we like
Kiss a friend on the cheek
Learn to listen to them
Make them a cake
Never be cross
Open your heart to them
Play a song and sing along
Quietly pulling funny faces to make them laugh
Remember them in our prayers
Share your toys to make someone happy
To hold their hand
Use a hug and give them a squeeze
Visit a friend to say hello
Writing them a story
Xxx's added at the end of a letter

You can always try and make them laugh
Zoom around on your scooter having fun

***

Helena Waxman
Age 5
Buckinghamshire, UK

126. Phoebe

What 'Kindness' Means to Me

Kindness can work for friends, family and strangers. Like helping someone when they're hurt or if they dropped something or even helping them chose something (e.g. book from the shop).

To be kind you need a heart and have the confidence to go up to someone and ask if they need help. Also, to be kind, you can compliment someone on what they're wearing or something they have achieved, like a painting or something they won.

I've helped a lot of people when they're hurt; what I have found is when you help someone it makes their day a lot better.

Being kind can be as simple just smiling at friends or a stranger, and it makes them smile back when they're not feeling the best they could ever be.

Kindness isn't something that you do when you feel like it, it is something that takes no effort and can be practised all the time.

Kindness makes people feel good about themselves and each other, but most of all it makes everyone feel good!

If everyone was kind in the world, it would be a happier place for people to be in and there wouldn't be any arguing!

Kindness can change people from grumpy into happy, happy, then into amazing. If everybody practised 'Kindness' in the world, the people in the world would be happier, more loving and would look after the environment even more.

"Kindness is a language that the deaf can hear and the blind can see."
– Mark Twain.

***

Phoebe Kerins
Age 9
Cheshire, UK

127. Martha

We need kind friends so we can cuddle them and play with them.
Being kind is helping.
At school we say kind feet, kind hands and kind words.
I like being kind all the time.
Being kind is giving stuff to people like toys and sweets.
Sharing my toys is kind.

***

Martha Spiby
Age 4
West Midlands, UK

128. Georgia

Kindness makes you live your life

Once upon a time, there lived a girl called Elizabeth. She was beautiful and tall. She loved to be kind and helpful and treat others the way she wanted to be treated.

One day, a boy said, "You're not allowed in my gang because you're a girl." The girl answered, "I'm just going to be the bigger person and treat you the way I want to be treated."

Elizabeth just went and found another group of boys and they were kind to her; they treated her how they wanted to be treated. The boy's names were Tim, Thomas, Tom, Taylor, Jacob, Ben and James. Elizabeth's other friends were Tilly, Isobel, Lilly, Tegan, Samantha and Isla.

They were really good friends with Elizabeth, so everybody was kind and happy.

All Elizabeth friends went on rollercoasters, to zoos, waterparks, sleepovers and on holidays with Elizabeth and their hearts were filled with kindness.

Elizabeth and her friends lived their lives with joy, kindness, smiles, giggles and happiness.

By the time they were adults they were all living together in a massive house with a massive garden and eight bedrooms.

***

Georgia Helen Kelly
Age 9
Lincolnshire, UK

129. Nate

Mum always tells me that it is important to always be nice and kind to people because we never know what they are going through. Kindness to me is:

Kindness makes Happiness
I like telling people I love them
Never breaking someone's heart
Doing things to help other people
Needing to help without expecting anything
Everybody deserves to be loved
Someone's feelings always matter
Showing you care

I show kindness by playing with everyone and inviting them to my birthday party and helping my friend who got stung by a bee. It made me feel special.

I know when I am kind and when someone is kind to me, it makes us happy and it feels good. If we are not kind to people then they will be sad and that is not very nice.

Mum asked me if I think we should be kind just to get something in return. I said no because kindness comes from the heart and shouldn't hurt people's feelings.

When mum asked me how I thought kindness changed the world I told her that if everyone was naughty and not kind, it would not be a very nice place to live and people would be mean to each other and everyone would be sad and there would be no happiness.

Happiness to me is being kind to people and people being kind to me. This is when I'm happy.

***

Nate Garcia
Age 5
Sydney, Australia

130. Quentin

Kindness is great
I like being kind, it makes me feel warm inside
Never miss an opportunity to be kind to someone
Doing something kind can make people smile
Nice is the same as kind
Expressing kindness is important to me
Sometimes it is nice to be kind to strangers
Sometimes you smile when you have been kind

***

Quentin Reynolds
Age 10
Nottinghamshire, UK

131. Megan

Megan's Song About Her Kindness Experience

I helped someone when he dropped his hat under his car
I helped someone when he dropped his hat under his car
I helped someone when he dropped his hat under his car

I picked it up for him
I picked it up for him
I picked it up for him

He was kind like me
He was kind like me
He was kind like me

I was nice to him too
I was nice to him too
I was nice to him too

He gave me a reward
He gave me a reward
He gave me a reward

***

Megan Reynolds
Age 7
Nottinghamshire, UK

132. Joseph

Learning to Be Kind

Sam was VERY unkind!

Sam was unkind because, as a toddler, he lived with his daddy, who was VERY unkind. He lived with his daddy because his mummy was in hospital for a whole year.

Sam learnt to be quite unkind, because this was all he saw.

Since 1996 (when Sam was 9), 27th February was known as 'Kindness Day', when everybody had to be kind for the whole day. The kindest person won a prize from the Government.

On Kindness Day, Sam saw everyone being kind, and everybody gave little presents to people who were being kind to them. Now, he didn't decide to be kind because it was a good thing to do, he only did so to get those presents! Everybody knew this, so nobody gave him any!

Then, he had a flashback to 27th February 1989 and remembered his daddy saying one sentence. This was, "The only reason I have been unkind for the whole of your life is because my dad was unkind and only one day ago, I realised this was wrong. So please don't listen to me son, just be kind, and listen to your mummy instead".

Sam thought about that sentence again and again and realised that being kind without expecting anything in return made you feel good, so from that day forward Sam became the kindest person in the world.

Oh, and he always won the prize on Kindness Day!

***

Joseph M. Rodenby
Age 9
Nottinghamshire, UK

133. Macie

Kindness is an action that can really make you feel great! There are different ways of expressing kindness. Our actions when we are around people are important. If we are aware of someone when they are sad or need help then practicing kindness is a great way to make both you and that other person feel good. There are less fortunate people out there and when we donate money or time out of our day to help them, that is a high level of kindness.

Kindness can also be how we treat our planet. We show kindness almost every day when we recycle or compost. Solar, recycling, giving a gift, planting new trees, and sharing are all great ways of practicing kindness.

Unfortunately, the world could still use more people who show kindness every day. Take the time to help friends or help the planet, jump starting your everyday kindness routine!

***

Macie Lee Griffin
Age 11
California, USA

134. Aaron

Kindness Is Easy

"Kindness is easy because it can be done by just smiling at somebody or helping them".

Tip, tap, chin, let our story about kindness begin…

Once upon a time, a kind boy called Aaron had a wonderful Christmas with his family. They had a lot of fun playing with all the new presents they got and eating all the Christmas food.

At night they cuddled on the sofa watching lots of movies together.

A few days later, Aaron's mummy asked him and his brother if they could sort their old toys so they could give some to other children.

Aaron said, "But, I like my toys, so I want to keep them."

"Hhhmmmm", said Aaron's mummy, "You had a lovely Christmas with new toys, but some children didn't even have food, heating or toys on Christmas day."

Aaron felt really sad and said, "Ok Mummy, I will give the children some of my toys and we can buy them some heaters to keep them warm and I have some money in my wallet to buy them some food."

Aaron's mummy asked if he, his brother and sister

would like to raise money to buy food for the foodbank and new toys for the children, so they were happy and shouted, "YES".

The next day that is what they started to do. All their family and friends were proud of them and wanted to help them to help others.

Four leaf clover, our story is over.

***

Aaron Elliott Jenson Mayers
Age 5
Cheshire, UK

135. Jess

Without Kindness, Everything Would Go Wrong

Kindness, kindness,
Doctors and parents give kindness,
Dentists and teachers give kindness.

Doctors help to make you better,
Parents give you all you need,
Dentists keep your teeth healthy and
Teachers help you to succeed.

If no kindness, what goes wrong?
There won't be friends to cheer you along,
People will only care about themselves,
No one to help if someone yells.

***

Jess Deane
Age 8
West Yorkshire, UK

136. Royal

Kindness is when my sister helps me with puzzles. It is also kind when Daddy plays blocks with me. It is not kind when my friends at school don't share. I am kind when I help Mom clean the house. I love being kind.

***

Royal Lynn Griffin
Age 3
California, USA

137. Caelan

Kindness is to be kind to one another and say nice words. Don't keep secrets from other people because that's not nice. Be nice to your friends and if someone gets hurt you help them up. Or if someone is running to the toilet and they fall over and graze their knee and are bleeding, you take them to the teacher and take them down to sick bay so they can get an icepack. When someone bullies you, say, "That's not nice" and they will say, "Sorry"; if they don't say sorry tell the teacher. Bullying makes you feel sad, so you tell the teacher and they can say sorry. You can be kind to say please don't bully anymore as you are being very rude.

Kindness is saying kind words. Kinds words you can say to people are, "Are you ok?" when they fall over. Also, saying nice words when someone gives you something such as please, thank you, may I, can I please, can I please do this for you?

I took everything off the table for Mummy and washed them and put them in the dishwasher. It's kind to do things for other people. I'm kind to my sisters by being nice to them. I show kindness by being kind, respectful and responsible.

***

Caelan Mulholland
Age 6
Sydney, Australia

138. Willow

Kindness is being nice to people and my Mummy because I love her.

Being kind is being nice to Mummy and my brother and sister, and when Daddy says home time I come straight away. I help Mummy get her drink bottle when she forgets it. I also give Mummy flowers and chocolate to be kind and give her cuddles and hugs.

I am nice to my sister by sharing my toys with her. I am respectful. I like my friends and I share with them and I also invite them to my birthday party.

I am kind by helping Daddy do the dishes. I helped my friend get in the sandpit.

***

Willow Mulholland
Age 4
Sydney, Australia

139. Aislinn

- Sharing
- Lying down at yoga (kindness to ourselves/ mindfulness)
- Kind to people
- Not be naughty
- Be kind
- Not throw things or sticks
- Giving Mum a kiss and cuddle

***

Aislinn Mulholland
Age 2
Sydney, Australia

What Does Kindness Mean to You?

Behind The Book

Child Author Project was founded by Jessica Prime
Illustrations and artwork by Kate Worrall
Typeset, formatting and cover design by Jen Parker

Jessica Prime

Jessica Prime is a best-selling author and advocate, and founder of Child Author Project.

Born in South Wales, UK, Jessica Prime is a mother to Seren, partner to Matthew and a trustee for Faye Knowles Chapman Foundation, campaigning to lower the age for cervical screening and advocating for cervical health awareness and education.

Jessica has been writing poetry, stories and content from a young age, first published in 2001, in a children's poetry collection.

Jessica has a fierce passion for mental health awareness and creating positive opportunities for children. Child Author Project was born to show children that they are capable of achieving amazing things with a little bit of hard work and some creativity.

Website: www.jessicaprime.co.uk
Website: www.childauthorproject.com

Follow Jessica on Facebook and Instagram:
@childauthorproject and @jessicaprimeva

Kate Worrall

Kate Worrall is a freelance Concept Artist and Illustrator based in Cheshire, UK. From a young age, Kate developed a passion for creating artwork, and studied Fine Art at College. At Teeside University, Kate merged an interest for art and games, studying Games Art and achieving First Class honours. Kate turned her passion and ambition into a successful business.

Predominantly working in Digital software, Kate is known for her ability to create a unique array of styles, from cartoon vector to detailed paintings. Her core passion remains deep rooted in fantasy style characters. During Kate's career, she has worked on a selection of projects, game art, illustrations, educational material and character branding, working with esteemed clients including Audible and Strand Magazine.

Website: www.kateprime.co.uk

Follow Kate on Facebook and Instagram:
www.facebook.com/TheArtworkOfKatePrime
www.instagram.com/kateprime.artist

Jen Parker

Jen is a mum to two girls aged three and one, with whom she loves reading beautiful books. She is married to Aaron and lives in Leicester with her family, including her little pooch, Doug, a pug crossed with a shih tzu. She runs the multi-award-winning Fuzzy Flamingo and is an editor and graphic designer specialising in book production, working from her home office.

If you'd like to get in touch with Jen about a forthcoming project, then you can do so via the following:

Website: www.fuzzyflamingo.co.uk
Email: contact@fuzzyflamingo.co.uk

Follow Jen on Facebook and Instagram:
@FuzzyFlamingoDesign

Our Ambassadors

An extra special thanks to our team of ambassadors who are supportive, encouraging and absolutely wonderful.

Chelle Clarke
Head of UK

Claire Clements
Essex

Emily Heather
Devon

Kris Davies
South Wales

Laura Bland
Leicestershire

Laura Young
Nottinghamshire

Mo Frances
Lanarkshire

Sarah Auger
Merseyside

Serena Novelli
Surrey

www.childauthorproject.com/team

Printed in Poland
by Amazon Fulfillment
Poland Sp. z o.o., Wrocław

57632492R00139